## DATE DUE

| | | | |
|---|---|---|---|
| JUN 3 1990 | MAR 15 | AUG 06 | |
| JUN 1 4 1990 | MAR 16 | | |
| JUN 2 8 1990 | APR 08 | | |
| JAN 0 6 1990 | OCT 8 | | |
| APR 1 4 1991 | DEC NOV 22 | | |
| MAY 2 2 1991 | | | |
| DEC 1 0 1991 | | | |
| DEC | | | |

243.1
HUB
#7016

Hubbard, David Allan.
   Unwrapping your
spiritual gifts.

$10.99

| DATE DUE | BORROWER'S NAME | ROOM NUMBER |
|---|---|---|

243.1
HUB
#7016

Hubbard, David Allan.
   Unwrapping your spiritual
gifts.

$10.99

# UNWRAPPING YOUR SPIRITUAL GIFTS

# UNWRAPPING YOUR SPIRITUAL GIFTS

## David Allan Hubbard

**WORD BOOKS**
PUBLISHER
WACO, TEXAS

A DIVISION OF
WORD, INCORPORATED

Library of Congress Cataloging-in-Publication Data

Hubbard, David Allan.
    Unwrapping your spiritual gifts.

    1. Gifts, Spiritual.  I. Title.
BT767.3.H8   1985        234'.13        85–12092
ISBN 0–8499–0478–1
Printed in the United States of America

# Contents

5

# Introduction

Determining God's call on one's life is sometimes a difficult and confusing task. How do we know what God wants us to do in service for him? How do we sort through the advice we receive from others? One person may tell us that we must have a mystical experience that reveals God's call. Another may say we should look at the needs around us—whatever needs to be done constitutes the call for us.

But these answers fail to take into consideration the key to determining God's call. The best indicator of what God wants us to do is in the equipment he has given us to use. Created in his image, each of us has special talents and abilities, a unique genetic composition, and emotional and psychological factors that make us individuals. And each of us, as Christ's person, has the Holy Spirit who brings his own special spiritual aptitudes into our lives. By looking at these characteristics and asking the question, "What do I do well?" we can begin to see God's call. We will have criteria with which to judge the many needs that beg for attention and be able to choose to work and serve in the areas where we can do our best.

How do you discover the gifts God has given you? There are lists of gifts in the New Testament which will give you clues. You can enlist others who know you well to give you an outside opinion of your strengths. Once your gifts are unwrapped, you can begin to put them to work. God's Spirit will enable and empower the use of these gifts to accomplish his purposes in you, in the church, and in the world.

Gifted persons have contributed to the usefulness of this book. Russell Spittler, Director of the David J. Duplessis Center for Christian Spirituality at Fuller, has offered several suggestions for improvement and Steven Pattie, my administrative assistant, has coordinated the final editing.

DAVID ALLAN HUBBARD

Every one to whom much is given,
of him will much be required. . . .

# 1

## Gifts and Their Giver

*Do not be deceived, my beloved brethren. Every good endowment and every perfect gift is from above, coming down from the Father of lights with whom there is no variation or shadow due to change. Of his own will he brought us forth by the word of truth that we should be a kind of first fruits of his creatures.*

*James 1:16–18*

Think how you would feel if this happened to you. For the past ten years you have sent a Christmas gift to a friend in a distant city. You have warmly cherished that friendship, and you have keenly respected the taste of your friend. Hence every Christmas gift you chose with exquisite care. Each gift was different from the other, and each was unique—hand crafted by master artisans throughout the world.

Beyond that careful shopping, you had paid detailed attention to how each was wrapped. Choice paper, fine ribbon, delicate bows—these adorned the gift as further testimonies to your depth of regard for the loved one.

Then how would you feel if this happened? After those joyful memories of ten Christmases, you are finally able to visit that friend. One thing that you look forward to is seeing the way in which your gifts have been put to work to grace and beautify the home. Yet when you finally arrive you see none of them in sight—no china vase on the piano, no brass candle-

13

sticks on the mantle, no hand-painted tile used as a trivet.

Finally your curiosity gets the best of you, and you peek in the storage closet. To your dismay you can count ten beautifully packaged gifts on the center shelf—each still unopened.

If you can sort out the range of sharp feelings that scene would evoke, you can begin to imagine how God feels about most of his people. He has given us meticulously chosen and eminently useful gifts, and we have left them unopened. It would not be too much to say that history's greatest untapped resource is the spiritual gifts the Lord of the churches has bestowed on his loved ones. It is time we unwrapped the gifts of God that we possess.

The first thing we need to do is to remind ourselves that they are *God's* gifts. A look at the Giver must precede an investigation of the gifts. Perhaps James' familiar words are the place to begin: "Do not be deceived, my beloved brethren. Every good endowment and every perfect gift is from above, coming down from the Father of lights with whom there is no variation or shadow due to change. Of his own will he brought us forth by the word of truth that we should be a kind of first fruits of his creatures" (James 1:16–18). Though this picture of God's magnificent generosity embraces more than the specific gifts of the Spirit listed in passages like Romans 2, 1 Corinthians 12, Ephesians 4, and 1 Peter 4, it surely includes them. They are an expression of the constancy of God's grace—they are part of the renewal that he wants to bring to the world he has made. One facet of Satan's great plan of deception is to lull us into leaving them unopened.

**14**     One of the ways to fight this deception is to remember that God is the Giver of these gifts. To help us do this we shall look at three great realities which the Bible makes clear as it teaches us about the One who makes all gifts possible: 1) God's pattern as Giver; 2) God's presence as Giver; 3) God's purpose as Giver. Let's see what God's Word has to say about each of these.

## God's Pattern As Giver

From Genesis to Revelation God is portrayed as the Giver. He is God of the generous heart, God of the open hand. His first great gift and his continuing legacy is the creation—he is *the Giver of life to creation:*

> These (the creatures of land and sea) all look to thee,
>     to give them their food in due
>     season.
> When thou givest to them, they
>     gather it up;
>     when thou openest thy hand, they
>     are filled with good things.
> When thou hidest thy face, they are
>     dismayed;
>     when thou takest away their breath,
>     they die
>     and return to their dust.
> When thou sendest forth thy Spirit,
>     they are created;
>     and thou renewest the face of the
>     ground
>
> (Psalm 104:27–30).

God is the *living* God, the only being in all the universe who is the source of his own life. All creatures—angels, animals, plants, human beings—live be- **15** cause of the gift of his life and because of that gift alone. Shut off that life, and the world would be deader than a doornail.

Our God is a Giver not only in the realm of creation but also in the arena of history—he is *the Giver of direction to history:*

> Say among the nations, "The Lord
>     reigns!
> Yea, the world is established, it
>     shall never be moved;
> he will judge the peoples with
>     equity."
> Let the heavens be glad, and let the
>     earth rejoice;
>     let the sea roar, and all that fills it;
>     let the field exult, and everything
>         in it!
> Then shall all the trees of the wood
>         sing for joy
>     before the Lord, for he comes,
>     for he comes to judge the earth.
> He will judge the world with righteousness,
>     and the peoples with his truth
>
> (Psalm 96:10–13).

God reigns, God comes, God judges—these exclamations proclaim his lordship. The peoples on every continent and the events of every century he uses to get his will done and to work out his purposes. His grace and judgment give human history its overall direction.

The rescue from sin and meaninglessness which the world so desperately needs is also a gift of God—*he is the Giver of salvation:*

**16**

O sing to the Lord a new
    song,
  for he has done marvelous things!
His right hand and his holy arm
    have gotten him victory.
The Lord has made known his
    victory,
  he has revealed his vindication in
    the sight of the nations.
He has remembered his steadfast
    love and faithfulness
  to the house of Israel.
All the ends of the earth have seen
    the victory of our God

(Psalm 98:1–3).

No salvation without God's gift—that is the biblical word. Part of it at least. The other part has been put this way: "For God so loved the world that he gave his only Son, that whoever believes in him should not perish but have eternal life" (John 3:16). As history's most lavish Giver, God climaxes his giving by the gift of his Son. He spared nothing; he gave his best. Our understanding of his spiritual gifts begins here: they are part of his process of bringing life, direction, and salvation to the human family. Since the greatest Giver sends them and they are among his good and perfect gifts, we unwrap them with delight and put them to work with enthusiasm.

## God's Presence As Giver

When we speak of God, all illustrations break down. His grace is too varied, his pattern of giving too splendid, to be embraced in any human illustration of giving—Christmas or otherwise. Not only did he give his Son, an act of love that defies illustration, but he him-    17 self comes to his people in the person of the Holy Spirit, who is his gift to all who have declared their full loyalty to him in repentance and faith.

To put it pointedly: *the Giver and the gift are one.* All who truly turn from their sins and believe that Jesus is God's Son and their Savior have the Holy Spirit. In fact, it is he who makes such turning possible; it is he who enables our hard hearts and blind eyes to know and see God's truth.

With the gift—singular—of the Spirit come the gifts—plural—of the Spirit. God, in other words, is not doing his work by remote control, sending signals from some heavenly transmitter. He is present within us—coaching us, encouraging us, equipping us, empowering us in our service for him.

### God's Purpose As Giver

God—the God who came to earth in his Son and dwells within us in his Spirit—is the Giver of spiritual gifts. He has done this for his special purposes, just as he has done everything else from the dawn of creation until now.

We must not miss what these purposes are. Because God is the Giver, *we can call his gifts good.* The "very good" with which he described his daily acts of creation in the beginning (Genesis 1) is the verdict that can be applied to all of God's gifts. They are "from above," as James taught us. They are part of the "every good endowment and every perfect gift" which he mentioned. The One who sends them is utterly brilliant and fully consistent—"the Father of lights with whom there is no variation or shadow due to change." God's gifts are called good because they are *purposeful.* No triviality or trifling, no frivolity or frills here— God's gifts are given to us purposefully. And their

18

purpose is to fulfill his purpose—winning men and women to faith in him and planting them solidly in that faith.

Because God is the Giver, *we can count on his gifts to work.* His gifts are expressions of his power and presence. When he spoke those powerful words of creation, "Let there be light!" did light have any choice not to be (Genesis 1:3)? When he stretched out his hand to cleave the sea, did it dare not split to let his people through (Exodus 14:21)? When he sent fire from heaven at Elijah's prayer, did the slaughtered sacrifices have the option not to burn (1 Kings 18:38)? God's gifts are *effective.* They are the work of his own Spirit through his people bringing holy change to human life.

Because God is the Giver, *we must treat his gifts with full seriousness.* They are not toys to amuse us on rainy afternoons. They are not heirlooms to be dusted and admired in a tidy cabinet. They are not trophies to display our prowess.

The Lord of creation, history, and salvation gives them as his way of including us in his work. As such his gifts are *essential.* Oh, he would get his work done another way if he were forced to. After all, he is God. But this is the way he has chosen. The Giver of all good gifts is a person who has enabled us as persons to do spiritual good in the lives of other persons.

It is high time to check the shelves of our lives for any unused gifts. Nothing would benefit the church of Jesus Christ, nothing would delight the heart of the Giver of life more than a huge unwrapping party. We are all invited.

# 2

---

# Gifts As Keys to Ministry

*Now there are varieties of gifts, but the same Spirit; and there are varieties of service, but the same Lord; and there are varieties of working, but it is the same God who inspires them all in every one. To each is given the manifestation of the Spirit for the common good.*

*1 Corinthians 12:4–7*

It is easy for us to underestimate the importance of God's gifts. Especially is this a temptation in our affluent society. As our standard of living has risen, the gifts we give to each other tend not to be essentials. Our Christmas gifts do not consist of sacks of potatoes, a six-month supply of bread, a certificate to repair the roof, or a drum of gasoline for the car.

Instead we buy for each other necklaces, cufflinks, artbooks, rare glass, or candlesticks. We treasure these gifts by wearing them on special occasions or displaying them in prominent places. They enrich our lives by their beauty, and they remind us of the loving care with which they were chosen. But we could do without them. They are not crucial to our daily needs or the survival of our families.

It would be easy for us to be misled just at this point. Because we think of gifts as embellishments, not as essentials, we can readily misunderstand what God's spiritual gifts are for. We may count them as enriching but not vital, as supplementary but not foun-  **23** dational. We may view them as additives to Christian life and mission like fluorides in toothpaste or ethyl in gasoline.

This would be a great mistake. God's spiritual gifts are his way of getting his work done; they are the means that he has chosen to fulfill his mission in the world through us, his people.

The illustration of the Christmas or birthday gifts is not a full description of how God has worked. Let us try another—let us suppose a wealthy person wanted to settle a new frontier, open up a vast area of previously uninhabited, unfarmed territory. At hand to do this with him was a large company of willing partners who lacked only one thing—they had no money. They wanted to be part of that lavish project but could contribute nothing to it but themselves.

Then suppose that the wealthy manager began to give them gifts to enable them to take part. Chainsaws to fell the timber, bulldozers to clear the land, lumber and concrete for houses and barns, plows and tractors to till the ground, seed and seedlings for the farms and orchards, fertilizer and irrigation equipment for the nurture of the crops, harvesters and trucks to cut and haul them—these were his gifts. Not a frill in the lot, not an item for ornament or decoration. Each was essential to the project; used together they made success possible.

Something like that is what God's spiritual gifts mean. They are a key to his ministry. They are the equipment that he has given us to accomplish his world-wide project of making his name known, of calling people everywhere to repentance and faith, of nurturing them to worship him in the fellowship of his church.

24　　To gain a larger picture of what God is doing and

how we fit, we need to see three things: (1) God's program of working in the world; (2) the world's most basic needs; (3) the Spirit's equipment to meet these needs. The master Farmer wants to sow his seed of life and truth throughout the world; he wants us to help; and he gives us vital, indispensable means to do so. Let us see how.

## God's Program in the World

Right from the beginning God has wanted the human family to cooperate in his work. To do this, he gave us the *gift of his image* so that we could do his will: "So God created man in his own image, in the image of God he created him; male and female he created them. And God blessed them, and God said to them, 'Be fruitful and multiply, and fill the earth and subdue it; and have dominion over the fish of the sea and over the birds of the air and over every living thing that moves upon the earth'" (Genesis 1:27–28). Those two verses make it plain: we were made like God in order to help him in his work of running the world. His gift had a purpose—our cooperation in his mission.

Later, after Adam's fall had divided the human family, turned it against itself and against God, God gave the *gift of his covenant* so that we could spread his light. To Abraham and his descendants he promised blessing as they served and worshiped him. By that service and worship they were to let the world know about the one true God—who he is, what he gives and what he requires.

Much later, when Abraham's family had settled in their God-given land, set up their God-ordered kingdom, and faltered in their God-mandated responsibili-   25 ties, God gave us another gift—the *gift of his presence*—so that we could teach all nations to love him. Jesus came. And in his life, death, and resurrection, he made it possible for men and women everywhere to know God, because Jesus was God's presence among us. Even when he left he pledged his constant presence to us as we carry his gospel throughout the earth: ". . . and lo, I am with you always, to the close of the age" (Matthew 28:20).

We see the persistence of God's purpose in the world. He gave gifts to his people—the gifts of his image, his covenant, his presence—for one reason: that we may carry out his works. His gifts are keys to his ministry. They are not incidental details; they are essential equipment for carrying out his will.

*The World's Basic Needs*

We can see how crucial the gifts of God's Spirit are if we view them from another angle. What kind of help does the world need? What are the basic problems that people face who have not yet come to worship God?

These questions are plainly answered in this description of paganism from the letter to the Ephesians: "Now this I affirm and testify in the Lord, that you must no longer live as the Gentiles do, in the futility of their minds; they are darkened in their understanding, alienated from the life of God because of the ignorance that is in them, due to their hardness of heart; they have become callous and have given themselves up to licentiousness, greedy to practice every kind of uncleanness" (Ephesians 4:17–19).

How are the work of God and the Word of God

to break into that bleak and clouded scene? *Spiritual understanding* is one basic need of persons who do not know Christ. What can bring that spiritual understanding to shatter the ignorance and callousness of their hearts? More education? I doubt it. Some of the most hardened sinners wear the robes and hoods of the best education centers in the world. Better taste? I do not think so. Spiritual discernment is not gained like art appreciation by strolling through great museums that portray the works of God's saints.

Who can bring that missing spiritual insight? Only the Spirit of God. No one else has the power to help us face up to our sin and see that Christ is the only Savior. He it is who plants God's own truth to flourish in us where the weeds of doubt and unbelief have thrived: "Therefore I want you to understand that no one speaking by the Spirit of God ever says 'Jesus be cursed!' and no one can say 'Jesus is Lord' except by the Holy Spirit" (1 Corinthians 12:3).

Spiritual understanding is one basic need; *spiritual power* is the other. Without it uncleanness is our natural state. We are drawn to the lewd, the immoral, the wicked until God's Spirit changes our wills, alters our values, and gives us power to lead lives of purity. Nothing else, no one else, can help us live on God's terms but God himself working in us.

The spiritual gifts, given to God's people as they entrust their lives to him, are keys to ministry. No other way can the basic needs of the world be met. God, the mighty land Owner, is seeking to build communities that will do his work, harvest his crops, erect his cities. And he does this in a world marked by ignorance and uncleanness. The struggle is not political, economic, social, or intellectual primarily, but spiritual.    27

Through the gifts given to the people in his church, the Lord of the church is meeting the world's basic needs.

## The Spirit's Effective Equipment

Four separate lists of spiritual gifts are recorded in the letters of the New Testament. The detailed study of them will come later. For now we want to see how each of them describes a way in which God is equipping his people for ministry.

*Gifts for service* are noted in Romans 12—gifts like prophecy, teaching, exhortation, financial means, acts of mercy. "Having gifts that differ according to the grace given to us, let us use them" (Romans 12:6) was what Paul urged. Gifts are given to be put to work, not to be hoarded or idolized. Each of them represents something utterly necessary if Christian ministry is to be complete. They are God's way of impacting on people to change their lives for the better. Who would dare treat them lightly?

*Gifts for leadership* are described in Ephesians 4— gifts like apostles, prophets, evangelists, pastors and teachers. Here the focus is on those people whom God has given special equipment to help the rest of us carry on effective ministry. All of Christ's men and women are ministers. And among them, God has given gifts to some to get the rest of us ready for ministry. These gifts are irreplaceable. Without them the most important tasks of God will not be carried out. Here is what depends on these gifts of leadership: ". . . the work of ministry . . . building up the body of Christ . . . the unity of the faith . . . the knowledge of the Son of God . . . mature manhood . . . the measure of the stature of the fulness of Christ" (Ephesians 4:12–13). What is that list but the catalog of history's most precious goals? Who could be so stupid as to keep these gifts shelved?

*Gifts for power* are displayed in 1 Corinthians 12—gifts like the utterance of wisdom, the utterance of knowledge, faith, healing, working of miracles, prophecy, the ability to distinguish between spirits, various kinds of tongues, interpretation of tongues. Their purpose according to Paul is to equip God's people for "varieties of service" (1 Corinthians 12:5). The pain, the suffering, the ignorance, the deviltry in the world all need putting down. God's ministry is to do new things in this old world; in fact he wants to work within it a new creation. His gifts of power are part of that renewal. Who would be so bold as to brand them irrelevant?

*Gifts for stewardship* are depicted in 1 Peter 4—gifts like hospitality, speaking, serving. "Stewards of God's varied grace" was what Peter called each of us. We have received special grace from God not only in forgiveness of sin, but in fitness to serve him. Who can be so unfaithful as to sleep through this call to duty?

For ministry God has given each of us gifts. Ours, therefore, is a *humble* ministry. What we accomplish, God alone has made possible.

And ours is also a *shared* ministry. We do not carry its burden alone. We are part of a world-wide task force gifted and chosen to further God's purposes.

Finally, ours is an *assured* ministry. God's Spirit is carrying it out. In him there can be no failure.

# 3

## Gifts As the Call of God

*But I have made no use of any of these rights, nor am I writing this to secure any such provision. For I would rather die than have any one deprive me of my ground for boasting. For if I preach the gospel, that gives me no ground for boasting. For necessity is laid upon me. Woe to me if I do not preach the gospel! For if I do this of my own will, I have a reward; but if not of my own will, I am entrusted with a commission. What then is my reward? Just this: that in my preaching I may make the gospel free of charge, not making full use of my right in the gospel.*

*1 Corinthians 9:15–18*

**D**iscussions about God's call can be confusing. There seem to be so many approaches to the subject. How does God call? How can we tell his voice from the others—like pressure from friends or our own inclinations? Those questions have been answered in a number of ways by God's people.

For instance, *status determined the call* for many, especially in the Middle Ages. For sons of lower and middle class families, the ministry offered an opportunity for educational advance and financial security that was otherwise beyond their reach. Monastic life and the priesthood were so esteemed by the common people that many young people may have entered those vocations for the prestige they afforded. A call to ministry offered attractive status, a chance to move up in the world. Along with the law, it was a highly esteemed profession.

The drive for status produced, of course, a ministry with a strong secular orientation. The churches were often centers of power politics as much as spiritual concern. But the Spirit of God who never abandons his people began to move among them in a new way. He began to speak to persons about the need for piety, the yearning to hear his voice, the openness to his personal call.

As the Spirit spoke in such ways, revivals often broke out. John Wesley's ministry in England and George Whitefield's in America before the Revolutionary War would be examples. So would Dwight L. Moody's campaigns and Billy Graham's crusades in the nineteenth and twentieth centuries. One component of these revivals was an emphasis on personal, spiritual call to ministry. Men and women were encouraged to open their hearts to God's will for their lives.

In such cases, *a crisis often determined the call.* Young people would attend a prayer or testimony service where a strong challenge would be issued. As a result of being deeply moved spiritually, they would surrender their wills to the call of God for ministerial or missionary service. I well remember such an experience in my own life. I was about fourteen at the time and planning to be a lawyer. God's voice came to me clearly in a moment of spiritual decision during an evening service in our little church. That decision has helped to guide my life ever since.

But many Christian people have never been through such a crisis. And some of them have been tempted to use that absence of a dramatic call as an excuse not to serve God.

To combat this spiritual lethargy, some Christian leaders developed another approach to a call. They noted that the commands of Jesus to his followers seemed inclusive. They were ordered into the world 34 to preach and teach without being told specifically where to go. The whole church, in fact, was to carry out this ministry, not just those to whom God had spoken some strong personal word.

*The need determined the call,* not the desire for status or a spiritual crisis. Wherever people were without the Word of God, wherever paganism was still their condition, wherever poverty, ignorance, and disease ran rampant, there the people of God were needed. No sense in waiting for a personal nudge from God when the needs of the world were shouting for relief.

Though this approach made some sense, it still caused considerable frustration. The needs were many, pressing, and widespread. Which of the hundreds of needs will determine my call? How do I weigh one need against another? Which need am I best suited to help meet?

That last question pushes us on in our quest for the key to what determines a call. For what am I best suited? That is a crucial question. It reminds us that God's equipment, given to us through our talents and our spiritual gifts, may be our best single clue to what God wants us to do.

In other words, more than any other factors, *our gifts determine our call.* They are God's firm, persistent signals to us of his will for our lives. As such, they do three things that need the full consideration of God's people: 1) gifts convey a direction; 2) gifts carry an urgency; and 3) gifts confer an obligation. We need to look briefly at each of these statements and pray that God will use that look to help us understand his will.

*Gifts Convey a Direction*

*Call* is a word that we use frequently without an adequate sense of what it means in the Scriptures. Its    35 primary application is to us—as members of Christ's body. Paul wrote to the believers at Rome in these words: ". . . including yourselves who are called to belong to Jesus Christ" (Romans 1:6).

That is our true calling. We are called from our allegiance to the world's beliefs and values to belong to Christ and to follow him. "Called to be saints" is one way Paul described this central calling (Romans 1:7; 1 Corinthians 1:2). By this he means that God's call —with its incredible powers—has summoned us to a different kind of life, a life separated from our past wickedness and dedicated to fellowship with and service of God.

Just what form that service may take has to be determined by each of God's people. Some may experience a dramatic call as Paul did on the road to Damascus. Jesus met him there and commissioned him to be an apostle to the Gentiles. But relatively few of God's servants get knocked from their horses by a blinding vision of Jesus.

For some, the need at hand may help to extend God's call. If we come across situations that we can help with—a lonely neighbor who needs a word of comfort, a teacherless class to whom we can minister, a church project to which we can lend a hand—then we are called to help where we can. But our response to such needs is usually brief and temporary. It would be difficult to base our lives on meeting such short-term needs. We need more direction than the day by day or week by week emergencies that come our way.

This is where spiritual gifts come in. They convey some specific directions as to how we work out our calling. We are called first to belong to Christ; then we are called to serve him and his people. The first call comes to us as the Spirit speaks to our hearts through the Word of God. The second call comes as we, with the help of other Christians, discover what God has given us the ability to do well. What personal talents and spiritual gifts do we have? The answer to that question conveys a sense of direction to our lives.

If we are good at entertaining, meet people well, make them feel comfortable, help them express their feelings—especially their feelings about God and his relationship to them—then we probably have the gift of hospitality. That gift, in turn, instructs us in what God has called us to do. We know from that gift where we fit in God's program. We have one good clue, at least, as to the special service God wants us to render.

God's gift of spiritual equipment, more than spiritual crisis and special need, is the best single indicator as to what we should do with our lives. God's gifts are like a personal message to us. They say, "This is what I have given you ability to do well, and this is what I want you to do for me." There is no clearer way for us to get direction. If we understand this, we make good head-way in clarifying the confusion that so often surrounds the matter of a call.

*Gifts Carry an Urgency*

God's call is never a casual matter. It was not casual when he spoke to Abraham and commandeered him for his service (Genesis 12:1–3). Nor when he summoned Moses at the burning bush and sent him to Egypt to demand the release of the tribes of Israel (Exodus 3:1–12). God's call was surely not casual when Jesus ordered fishermen like James and John to leave their nets and go with him (Mark 1:18–20).

The spiritual gifts that God gives convey a direction for our lives. They tie us to his service and indicate    **37** how that service will express itself. In other words, the gifts are God's call to us. Because they are *God's* call, they carry an urgency that must be heeded.

That urgency is present in virtually every biblical passage where the gifts of the Spirit are described. Here are some samples: "Having gifts that differ according to the grace given to us, *let us use them*" (Romans 12:6). "But *earnestly desire* the higher gifts" (1 Corinthians 12:31). "As each has received a gift, *employ it* for one another, as good stewards of God's varied grace" (1 Peter 4:10). These are gifts of God's wise, loving, powerful Spirit. Use them; employ them; desire them. So stated are the apostolic commands.

No room here for casualness. A neglected gift, an unused ability is an affront to God, the gracious Giver. A call unheeded is an insult to God, the compelling Caller. He calls through his gifts; those gifts, therefore, carry an urgency.

*Gifts Confer an Obligation*

God's gifts are a personal call to us; they draw us into his work with direction and with urgency. The gifts and the call that comes through them are the chief ways in which God carries out his mission. As members of Christ's body, the church, answer their call and employ their gifts, the church is strengthened and the world is served. God's love is known; God's grace is demonstrated; God's name is honored.

These are life's most important tasks. They are the breath and blood of human existence. Nothing outranks them in importance; nothing can substitute for them. Knowing God's love, demonstrating God's grace, honoring God's name—those are the tasks for which we were called. Those are duties without which all living is finally failure.

38

So keenly did Paul feel the obligation which God's gifts conferred to him that he cried out, "Woe to me if I do not preach the gospel!" (1 Corinthians 9:16). God had called him and given him the gifts to be an apostle. This call and these gifts brought with them a compelling, an inescapable, obligation.

Mark how Paul expressed that obligation. Not "Woe to *the church and the world* if I do not preach . . . ," but "Woe to *me*. . . ." God's gifts put us under a personal obligation. If we do not use them, we are the losers. God in his sovereign majesty, God in his limitless power will raise up others to do the work. But he will hold us accountable for missing his purpose, for abusing his grace, for leaving his gifts unwrapped.

His call that comes through his gifts leaves us no option. We obey it, or else.

Three things we must remember as we ponder our place in all of this. The first is *Who gave the call*. We are face to face with the living God who has summoned us to join his company and serve in his mission.

The second thing to recall is *what is at stake*. We are in terrible danger of trifling with God's grace, of backing away from his purposes, of bringing woe on ourselves if we do not put our spiritual gifts at the use of him who gave them.

The third thing to keep in mind is *how to say yes*. The details of how will appear in later chapters. For now it is enough to say that we must be open to obey God and to move in the direction in which his gifts to us are pointing. That openness is the first great *yes* to God. The other specific *yesses* will follow as God makes known the details of our calling.

# 4

---

# Gifts and Their
# Discovery: Part One

*For by the grace given to me I bid every one among you not to think of himself more highly than he ought to think, but to think with sober judgment, each according to the measure of faith which God has assigned him. For as in one body we have many members, and all the members do not have the same function, so we, though many, are one body in Christ, and individually members one of another. Having gifts that differ according to the grace given to us, let us use them: if prophecy, in proportion to our faith; if service, in our serving; he who teaches, in his teaching; he who exhorts, in his exhortation; he who contributes, in liberality; he who gives aid, with zeal; he who does acts of mercy, with cheerfulness.*
*Romans 12:3–8*

I t is one thing to believe in spiritual gifts. It is another thing to know which gifts you may have.

So far in these chapters we have tried to set the stage by showing how the gifts of the Holy Spirit play an essential part in God's program. They are extensions of his hands, accomplishing his purposes; they are echoes of his voice, issuing his personal call to us.

Now it is time to see how that call comes to us. The story of Christ's church is the story of the use of spiritual gifts. We have come to the point where we must write our own names into the story, or, to put it more accurately, we must learn how God has written our names into that story.

God has called us from our relationship to the world and summoned us into his family. The sign of that family membership is the presence of his Holy Spirit within us. That Spirit—the very Spirit of the true and living God—does many things. He renews our lives to live on God's terms; he assures us that we belong to God; he chides us when we sin and gives us grace to repent; he ties us to the rest of God's people with an intimacy as close as organs of a body have to each other.

And the Holy Spirit brings with him his special gifts. He never comes without them. Every one who by faith in Jesus Christ, as the crucified and risen Lord, belongs to God's family is indwelt by the Spirit. And every one who has God's Spirit has some spiritual gift or gifts.

These gifts are not accessories to adorn God's work; they are instruments to accomplish it. They are not like the figurines on the kitchen shelf adding a touch of beauty; they are like the stove heating food to feed a hungry family. They are not the tuxedo which makes the cellist look elegant; they are the instrument through which heavenly music is produced.

God is never more serious than when he drafts us for his ministry. The gifts and the direction for our lives that comes with them are as vital to his program as was the call to Abraham, the command to Moses, the covenant with David (2 Samuel 7). Because God is serious, we must be. His strong call insists on our firm "yes." What God personally has given to us we must discover personally.

To help us do that, we shall look at one of the key passages listing some of God's gifts—Romans 12:3–8: "For by the grace given to me I bid every one among you not to think of himself more highly than he ought to think, but to think with sober judgment, each according to the measure of faith which God has assigned him. For as in one body we have many members, and all the members do not have the same function, so we, though many, are one body in Christ, and individually members one of another. Having gifts that differ according to the grace given to us, let us use them: if prophecy, in proportion to our faith; if service, in our serving; he who teaches, in his teaching; he who exhorts, in his exhortation; he who contributes, in liberality; he who gives aid, with zeal; he who does acts of mercy, with cheerfulness."

We want to say "yes" to God's gifts. That passage will help us discover what gifts we have and how to put them to work in God's service. Three guidelines need to be followed: 1) bear in mind the importance of gifts; 2) pour over the lists of gifts; 3) put to work any gift that may apply to you. God is waiting to help you find your place in his program. We want to give him full attention.

*Bear in Mind the Importance of Gifts*

Gifts are important because *they are for Christians.* Everybody you meet has some talents, some attractive personal qualities, some traits of character or skill of performance that make them special. Every member of the human family is a creature of God, and the grace of God's creative work has given each of them some natural gifts that enable him or her to make some contribution to society.

But spiritual gifts are special and different. They are given only to those in whom God's Spirit lives because they have committed themselves to Jesus as Lord and Savior. No person who is not a Christian has spiritual gifts, and every person who is a Christian has gifts. The whole context of Romans 12 underscores this. It is addressed to those who have experienced the mercies of God, who are dedicated to doing God's will, whom God has assigned a measure of faith, and who are members of Christ's body (Romans 12:1–5).

Ask yourself, then, about your relationship to     **45**

Christ. That is the first and most vital step in discovering spiritual gifts. They are for Christians. Are you one?

Gifts are important because *they are demonstrations of God's grace.* God has bent over to reach us; even more, he has come to us in his Holy Spirit. That is a magnificent expression of grace. We cannot trifle with that. When we do, we are tampering with the very heart of God. That is why Paul calls for "sober judgment" in the understanding of gifts and for diligence in the use of them (Romans 12:3,6). Discovery of our gifts begins as we bear in mind their importance.

*Pore Over the Lists of Gifts*

There are four main lists of gifts in the New Testament. We shall look at each of these in turn during the next few chapters. For now our focus is on the list of gifts in Romans 12. You may or you may not find your gifts there. But the exercise of asking yourself about them will give you practice and insight that you can then apply to the other lists of gifts.

The gift of *prophecy* is mentioned first, probably because it is so vital to the life of God's people. Prophecy as a spiritual gift involves two things: 1) a deep understanding of and belief in the truths of God— that is what Paul means by the phrase "in proportion to our faith" in Romans 12:6; and 2) a power to make that truth known to others with clarity and conviction.

The real test of the gift of prophecy is whether those who hear God's Word proclaimed are moved by it. When we think of this gift we may identify it with great preachers like Billy Graham, Leighton Ford, Oswald Hoffman, or John Stott. Undoubtedly these men of international stature have that gift. Their sermons move people to commit their lives to Jesus or to deepen their dedication to his gospel and his church.

But it is not only the famous who have this gift. What success have you had in persuading people to change their ways, to strengthen their spiritual walk, to follow Christ more closely? If you have seen lives changed, faith brightened, understanding opened, or commitment sharpened, then you may have the gift of prophecy. Treasure it, cultivate it, use it. It is God's way of moving his people forward in faith and mission.

The gift of *service* needs looking at. It comes next because it complements the gift of prophecy. God's truth comes to the world in both words and deeds. His love is to be talked about with spiritual power and demonstrated with practical clarity.

The Greek word for service is related to our word *deacon*. It refers to acts of love, kindness, and consideration done in ways that reflect God's own care. The first deacons took care of many practical and personal needs like helping the widows manage their lives after they had depended so heavily on their husbands.

Do you have the gift of service? Do you like to help others with their practical problems? Can you do it without being pushy or meddling? Do others receive your help with joy and thanksgiving? Can you keep on serving without frustration or bitterness? Those are the right questions. Service, by the way, is something that anyone can try. Do it and see what God's answer is.

The gift of *teaching* is needed in every congregation. It is essential for the understanding of God's ways. Christian faith is information as well as experience. The person who has the gift of teaching is one who grasps the truths of Scripture and has unusual facility in explaining, illustrating, and applying them.

47

My mother had the gift of teaching. You could tell that by the way people's faces brightened, their heads nodded in enthusiastic reception of the truth, and their lives changed from being curious spectators to becoming Christian disciples. All these things happened to people under her ministry.

Have you tried teaching? What has happened? Did people say, "I like that illustration. I never thought of that before. I'm going to try that in my own life"? Teaching is something that virtually every believer should give a test. Latent, unused gifts of teaching are present in every church. Maybe yours is among them.

The gift of *exhortation* can play a vital role. Discouragement and distress are found wherever God's people gather. Strength and comfort are never out of style. The need for them is constant.

Exhortation is a wonderful spiritual gift. It is an extension of the Holy Spirit's ministry as comforter or counselor. The Greek term *Paraklete,* one of the Spirit's titles (John 14:15–17), is directly related to the word for exhortation. It describes people who have the gift of saying what is needed in times of distress or emergency. They come alongside to help (as the Greek word suggests), and they say and do the right things. Their words encourage and strengthen us by reminding us of God's love and power.

The gift of *contributing* is easily overlooked. We think of the ability to earn money and give it away as the product of natural circumstances like an affluent family or a good head for business. Yet when we reflect for a moment, we can see what a spiritual gift it is. Who but the Spirit can help us break through our selfishness? Who but the Spirit can tell us of the importance of God's work? Who but the Spirit can prompt us to give without demanding credit or trying to control what we support?

The gift of *giving aid* is sorely needed in our painful world. Think of the ignorance, the loneliness, the lack of purpose, the spiritual and physical poverty around us. How good of God's Spirit to equip some people with unusual ability, time, and energy to spot these pains and help to ease them.

The gift of *acts of mercy* is similar. Those who have it are especially sensitive to the needs of the underdogs, the oppressed, the up-against-it. The demand for mercy is endless. The circumstances where it is most necessary are depressing. That is why Paul directed that this gift be employed with cheerfulness. Mercy rendered grudgingly is a drag to those who render it and a drug to those who receive it. Marvelously gifted are those who stoop to the weaknesses of others without making the others feel unnecessary.

## Put to Work Any Gift That May Apply

You will never know if you can do it until you try. And if you do not succeed try again. The old maxims apply to the exercise of spiritual gifts. If any of those gifts that Paul pinpointed sounds like you, look for opportunities to put the gift or gifts to work in your life.

*Remember how simple God's gifts may be.* It is easy for us to think of the most gifted people we know and demean ourselves in comparison with them. We cannot preach like Lloyd Ogilvie, teach like Roberta Hestenes, or make financial contributions like C. Davis Weyerhaeuser. As a result we assume that we have no gifts.

But the gifts may take less grandiose or dramatic    **49**

forms. We may contribute small amounts of money faithfully and wisely as a sign that we have the gift of contributing. Acts of mercy, aid to the needy, or ability to exhort and encourage others may be employed on a modest scale. After all, helping one or two or a handful of church members has great consequences before God. It takes the Spirit's work to do that well just as it does to perform Christ's work on a larger scale.

*Remember that God's gifts come in numbers large and small.* Because the Giver of gifts, God's Holy Spirit, is present in us, there is no limit to the number of gifts any Christian may possess. For that reason the discovery of our gifts takes patience. It may stretch over long periods of time—even years. Once we have identified a gift, we can joyfully put it to work while we keep our hearts and minds on the lookout for other gifts—in ourselves and in our fellow followers of Jesus.

*Remember that God's gifts do his kinds of work.* Take any gift on Paul's list, and you will note that the work done is just what God does—declaring his Word, teaching his people, serving their needs, giving generously of his resources, coming to the aid of the needy, and lavishing his mercy upon us with good cheer.

Discovering our spiritual gifts is not easy. But there is great incentive. Nothing will satisfy us more than to do what God has gifted us to do. Nothing will bring more joy than to do his kind of work in his kind of power.

# 5

---

# Gifts and Their
# Discovery: Part Two

*Now there are varieties of gifts, but the same Spirit; and there are varieties of service, but the same Lord; and there are varieties of working, but it is the same God who inspires them all in every one. To each is given the manifestation of the Spirit for the common good. To one is given through the Spirit the utterance of wisdom, and to another the utterance of knowledge according to the same Spirit, to another faith by the same Spirit, to another gifts of healing by the one Spirit, to another the working of miracles, to another prophecy, to another the ability to distinguish between spirits, to another various kinds of tongues, to another the interpretation of tongues. All these are inspired by one and the same Spirit, who apportions to each one individually as he wills.*
1 Corinthians 12:4–11

Some gifts of God's Spirit are more dramatic than others. *The gifts of power* listed in 1 Corinthians 12 are the most dramatic of all. Paul's catalog will sound strange to modern ears, especially to persons who have had little experience of pentecostal churches or the charismatic movement: "Now there are varieties of gifts, but the same Spirit; and there are varieties of service, but the same Lord; and there are varieties of working, but it is the same God who inspires them all in every one. To each is given the manifestation of the Spirit for the common good. To one is given through the Spirit the utterance of wisdom, and to another the utterance of knowledge according to the same Spirit, to another faith by the same Spirit, to another gifts of healing by the one Spirit, to another the working of miracles, to another prophecy, to another the ability to distinguish between spirits, to another various kinds of tongues, to another the interpretation of tongues. All these are inspired by one and the same Spirit, who apportions to each one individually as he wills" (1 Corinthians 12:4–11).      **53**

That set of gifts is so unusual, so dramatic, so beyond our natural powers, that one might guess it would be simple to discover whether one possessed them. In a sense that is true. But in another sense the matter is a bit more complicated.

These gifts, too, have to be tested. With *gifts of service*—like teaching, exhorting, contributing money, or showing mercy—the problem may be to distinguish the Spirit's work from our natural talents or inclinations. With *gifts of power*, the problem is different. They are public, visible gifts, readily displayed before other Christians. They differ sharply from normal human practices. Speaking in tongues, working miracles, healing the sick—these are not everyday activities for most people.

When such unusual events do occur, there are several possible explanations. First, God's Spirit may be at work; he has lost none of the power that he demonstrated in Jesus and the apostles. Second, demonic power may be in evidence; counterfeiting God's work is something Satan has been doing since the days when Pharaoh's magicians imitated some of Moses' miracles (Exodus 7:20–22). Third, psychic forces within a person may account for some of these activities; we are just beginning to recognize the profound psychological influences that some persons hold over others.

Discovering whether manifestations of power are truly gifts of the Spirit, then, takes some discernment. Happily, the very passage that describes these gifts gives us clues to determine their authenticity. Two basic steps need to be taken: first, evaluate your effectiveness in God's work; second, look for affirmation from God's people. Spiritual gifts are a key to God's ministry in the world and to our special calling within that ministry. Any effort that we make to test our

54

gifts and those of our fellow Christians will pay rich dividends in our service for Christ.

*Evaluate Your Effectiveness in God's Work*

Paul's instruction about these gifts of power begins with the assumption that some people may be led astray in using them: "Now concerning spiritual gifts, brethren, I do not want you to be uninformed. You know that when you were heathen, you were led astray to dumb idols, however you may have been moved. Therefore I want you to understand that no one speaking by the Spirit of God ever says 'Jesus be cursed!' and no one can say 'Jesus is Lord' except by the Holy Spirit" (1 Corinthians 12:1–3).

If we read between Paul's lines we gain the impression that some people in the Corinthian congregation were counterfeiting these gifts. Even worse, they were supposedly using the Spirit's power to pronounce curses on Jesus—to deny that he is God's Christ, our Lord and Savior. They were frauds and deceivers, as sharply separated from the true and living God as heathen idols are.

The first step, we can see, in evaluating our effectiveness in God's work is to look for *the celebration of Christ's lordship.* This would be particularly true in the gifts which express themselves in words. When an "utterance of knowledge" is given to someone in the congregation, is Jesus honored as Lord?

True knowledge in a biblical sense is always centered in Christ, for in him "are hid all the treasures of wisdom and knowledge" (Colossians 2:3). He it is who knows all the past and future and can read the present secrets of our hearts. He it is who discerns the mystery of the Father's working and can reveal it to us. Much of that was missed by the people at Corinth; they were tempted to interpret "knowledge" as a spiritual power that only a select elite enjoyed (1 Corinthians 8:2). Often that supposed power made them haughty and superior in their relationships with others, and, at times, it made them feel that they were even above God's principles of sexual morality and marital fidelity.

Such words were not an "utterance of knowledge" in any true sense. They did not elevate the Lord Jesus Christ. Specifically, the "utterance of knowledge" seems to refer to a word from God about the future or about some secret that a person is carrying that should be exposed. Michael Green, in his book *I Believe in the Holy Spirit*, suggests two biblical illustrations of this gift: Jesus' ability to tell that the Samaritan woman had lived with five husbands and a sixth man to whom she was not married (John 4:18); Peter's insight into the deception of Ananias and Sapphira who claimed to have brought to the apostles all the profit after selling a piece of property yet actually retained some for themselves (Acts 5:3–4). We note that in both of these cases, the use of the utterance of knowledge is to help people face their sinful situations and submit to Christ's lordship.

The "utterance of wisdom" is the God-given ability to give practical advice about Christian decisions and Christian living. It is a gift; it can take no credit for itself. It is Christ-centered because he is the source of true wisdom and his death for us on the cross is the greatest act of wisdom (1 Corinthians 1:23–24).

The three other gifts of speech—"prophecy," "various kinds of tongues," and "the interpretation of tongues"—must also celebrate Christ's lordship. Prophecy is inspired preaching, the clear declaration of God's truth in the unction of the Spirit. Who is

God's truth, but Jesus (John 14:6)? No words of Christian proclamation can really bear the Spirit's imprint unless they honor the Lord Jesus Christ.

In public worship, when speaking in tongues and the interpretation of them go hand in hand (as they must do in the biblical pattern, 1 Corinthians 14:27–28) together they form a kind of prophecy. The purposes of those gifts are 1) to convict unbelievers so that they will repent and believe in God and 2) to build up believers in faith, love, and holiness. It is obvious that neither of these purposes can be accomplished unless Jesus is honored as Lord. He is the One who leads us to God and who strengthens our confidence in him.

The Holy Spirit is the Spirit of Christ. He speaks to us of the ways and works of Christ. He draws us closer to Christ. He makes us more Christlike. No word or act—no matter how powerful it appears—is truly the work of the Spirit unless it enhances our reverence for Christ.

As we evaluate the effectiveness of our work or the work of others who claim to have gifts of the Holy Spirit, there is another step we must take: we must look for *the evidence of God's work*. Paul drilled this point home with words like these: "Now there are varieties of gifts, but the same Spirit; and there are varieties of service, but the same Lord; and there are varieties of working, but it is the same God who inspires them all in every one" (1 Corinthians 12:4–6).

The gifts come from the Triune God. Note Paul's mention of the Holy Spirit, the Lord (that is the risen Christ), and God (the Father). The gifts are designed to do *God's work*. That means they are helpful, not harmful; they are constructive, not destructive; they contribute to his program of salvation, not detract from it. This is particularly true of the gifts of wonder-working like faith, healing, and the working of miracles.

These gifts must be tested by the works of God themselves as recorded in Scripture. *Faith* must be faith to do good works, works like Jesus wrought when he lived among us. And it must be *faith in God,* not faith in the power of the person to do good works. The miracles are not magical rites; they are the work of God, done in his power, for his purpose, and for his glory.

God's work done in *his way*—that must be the principle that governs the correct use of spiritual gifts. Supposed acts of healing or miracles done through psychic or demonic power usually call attention either to the ritual—special words, ceremonies, or actions— or to the prowess of the wonder-worker. Where either the formula or the person holds the spotlight, God does not get the glory. Where God does not get the glory, the action cannot be right no matter how dramatic or effective it may seem.

God is a God of order and unity. His works will never contradict his Word. That means that conformity to Scripture is part of the evidence we use to test spiritual gifts. Any so-called prophecy, utterance of wisdom, or interpretation of speaking in tongues that urged Christians to engage in sexual immorality would be patently false. God's Spirit does not command chastity in Scripture and then contradict his Word through an alleged gift of the Spirit. Part of the "ability to distinguish between spirits" is knowing how to apply God's Word to supposed activities of his Spirit.

*Look for Affirmation from God's People*

The gifts need testing, especially those dramatic gifts of power that can be impressive. We test them in ourselves and others by checking their effectiveness in honoring Jesus as Lord and in doing works that God approves in ways that please him. We also test them by seeing what God's people say about them.

*"The common good"* was an important phrase in Paul's instruction. Gifts are for the whole body. They must be used only in ways that help others. My mother once rebuked a person who was engaged in some "spiritual" activity that distracted others and upset the tone of the prayer meeting. The person chided her: "Mrs. Hubbard, you are quenching the Spirit." My mother's reply was sharp and correct. "Yes, I'm quenching your spirit." The Spirit works for the common good. That person's distracting and unseemly behavior was out of bounds.

Are others helped? Is their devotion to Christ and obedience to his Word enhanced? Is the congregation strengthened in worship and aided in mission? Those are the kinds of questions to be asked. Gifts—especially these exuberant gifts mentioned in 1 Corinthians 12—are too heady and exhilarating to be exercised without the affirmation of the spiritually wise. Do not hesitate to consult with fellow believers whose holiness and wisdom you admire. There is safety in a multitude of such counselors.

The *"still more excellent way"* (1 Corinthians 12:31) is also part of the test of spirituality. It is no coincidence that Paul set his magnificent poem of love (1 Corinthians 13) between his chapters on the gifts of power. There like a jewel it shines—reminding us that in Christian terms character is worth more than activity; love outranks power and knowledge; how we care for God's people is more important than what we do in God's service.

If the gifts of the Spirit are exercised in pride, compe-    **59** tition, or conflict, they will not amount to much in God's sight no matter how we may value them. Love is the prime Christian reality; whatever crowds it out of the center of our lives must be set on the shelf until love can be restored.

Christians of all stripes need to hear afresh the call to love. The gifts of the Spirit, notably these gifts of power, have often plunged Christians into fierce controversy. One reason why God has spread his gifts around and given each of his people at least one is to make us cling together, depend on each other, respect each other. Far from setting off fierce competition, a chief purpose of the gifts is to draw us together in the community of the church. The gifts tell us that we desperately need each other. And love is the best way to express that need.

Persons who practice these gifts can become proud and pushy; they herald this particular list of gifts as the medicine for all human problems and as the badge of true spirituality. Persons who do not possess these gifts, in turn, have become defensive and hostile. They may denounce speaking in tongues as the work of the devil, without adequate biblical study.

Nothing good can come of such lovelessness. The gifts must be tested along the lines I have described to see whether God's Spirit is truly at work. But one thing is sure: nothing exposes his absence more clearly than lack of love. Our task of discovering God's gifts must not miss the greatest gift—the God-demonstrated ability to care for each other as his people, despite our differences.

# 6

## Gifts and Their
## Cultivation: Part One

*And his gifts were that some should be apostles, some prophets, some evangelists, some pastors and teachers, for the equipment of the saints, for the work of ministry, for building up the body of Christ, until we all attain to the unity of the faith and of the knowledge of the Son of God, to mature manhood, to the measure of the stature of the fulness of Christ; so that we may no longer be children, tossed to and fro and carried about with every wind of doctrine, by the cunning of men, by their craftiness in deceitful wiles. Rather, speaking the truth in love, we are to grow up in every way into him who is the head, into Christ, from whom the whole body, joined and knit together by every joint with which it is supplied, when each part is working properly, makes bodily growth and upbuilds itself in love.*

*Ephesians 4:11–16*

The note at the bottom of the church bulletin caught my eye. It listed the leaders of the congregation by name and office: pastor, minister of family life and education, junior and senior high ministries, ministers in music and the arts, secretary, and sexton. That list contained no surprises. Many churches have a staff of leaders with titles similar to those.

What caught my eye was the line that followed. Its phrasing was direct and simple: "plus 539 ministers." You get the point: the church is comprised of leaders with special duties and a whole congregation— 539 of them in that church—of ministers. We ministers in the congregation are Christ's servants. Our task is to do his work. We are his mouth, his hands, his feet. We speak of his love and then illustrate that speech by our care of others.

If that work—speaking and demonstrating Christ's love—is what all of us Christians do as ministers, then what do our leaders do? What about the pastor, the ministers of family life, youth, and music who are listed in the bulletin? Their task can be simply put: it is to lead, encourage, and enable the rest of us so that we can carry on the ministry.

Think how effective that pattern is. In a city like Pasadena, with more than a hundred thousand people within a fifteen-minute drive of our church, we need to touch the lives of several thousand persons every year. Could our half-dozen full and part-time leaders do that? Of course not—even if each of them met three new people a day. Our aim as a church is to make a difference, a big difference, in Pasadena. There is no way that we can do this unless each of the 539 members is a minister.

But this ministry is something we have to learn. It takes time, patience, talent, and good instruction. The last ingredient—good instruction—is where our leaders come in. They are called to shepherd us with their care and comfort so that we in turn can shepherd others. They are prepared to teach us what the Bible means and what it demands in order that we too can interpret our faith to those who do not know it.

This shepherding and this instructing are the two main responsibilities of church leaders today. To enable men and women to carry out these responsibilities, God's Spirit has equipped them with *gifts of leadership*. This is how the New Testament describes what these gifts are and how they work: "And his gifts were that some should be apostles, some prophets, some evangelists, some pastors and teachers (the shepherding and the instructing!), for the equipment of the saints, for the work of ministry, for building up the body of Christ, until we all attain to the unity of the faith and of the knowledge of the Son of God, to mature manhood, to the measure of the stature of the fulness of Christ; so that we may no longer be children, tossed to and fro, and carried about with every wind of doctrine, by the cunning of men, by their craftiness in deceitful wiles" (Ephesians 4:11–14).

Apostles, prophets, evangelists, pastors and teachers (one office, as we shall see)—those are the chief callings to leadership in the New Testament churches. Who has these gifts? How can we know that we have one of them, how do we cultivate it so that we can use the gift as effectively as God wants us to? Those are heavy questions. I can only begin to answer them.

Three steps need looking at: deciding, training, practicing. May the Spirit of God help many of us to find his will as we look at each of these areas.

*Deciding about Gifts of Leadership*

The chore of deciding which gift of leadership God has given to us has been made simpler for us nearly two thousand years after the church was founded than it was for those who were present at the beginning. Simpler, I say, because two of the four gifts seem to have ceased to play a dominant function once the church was founded and the Scriptures completed.

*Apostles* were the men who helped to found the church. A chief requirement for them was to have seen the resurrected Christ with their own eyes (1 Corinthians 9:1). What they had personally witnessed of Jesus' words and deeds they passed on to others.

Strictly speaking, there are no modern apostles. They did their work at the beginning. They did it well. The church has survived; the Christian message has been preserved. The Scriptures are known and loved around the world. Yet, in a sense, when men and women pioneer Christian work in unevangelized places and bring for the first time their witness to Christ's death and **65** resurrection, they are carrying out an apostolic mission. *Prophets* also played their part at the beginning. Before the Scriptures were fully written (about A.D. 100), the prophets brought special words of revelation, encouragement, and exhortation to the churches. After God's Word was recorded in its entirety, the Holy Spirit used the Scriptures which he had fully inspired to bring that prophetic instruction. Yet, on occasion, God may still raise up men and women of prophetic vision and courage in places where the planting of the church calls for special gifts. Whether with modern "apostles" or "prophets," the acid test of their ministry is fidelity to Christ and what is taught about him in the Scriptures. A safe rule-of-thumb today is to honor those persons who carry on apostolic or prophetic ministries without calling attention to themselves or seeking acclaim, and to beware of those leaders who publicly label themselves as apostles or prophets.

Apostles and prophets, then, did their work as God gave them gifts to do it. That founding ministry is no longer needed, especially where the church is well-founded. The basic Christian tasks of leadership are now in the hands of evangelists and pastor-teachers.

How can we decide if we have one of these gifts? One answer is *carefully*. James' words must be heeded: "Let not many of you become teachers, my brethren, for you know that we who teach shall be judged with greater strictness" (James 3:1). The responsibilities of spiritual leadership are weighty. We dare not rush into them.

To be a leader, one must have followers. This means that a decision about these gifts has to be made *corporately*. Others have to help us. We cannot decide by ourselves. I cannot walk into a roomful of Christians, straighten my tie, and announce, "I am your leader."

They must say to me, "You are our leader." Wise and loving followers of Christ must see us at work for him and help us decide whether we are truly equipped and called to preach the gospel to outsiders and encourage believers in their growth.

All of this means that the decision must be made *experientially.* We try what we think the Lord may be calling us to do. If the response is positive—if Christians respond to our teaching and counseling or if non-Christians accept our witness and open their lives to Christ—then our sense of call is being confirmed by our experience. God is at work in our lives in this special way.

Daniel Fuller's own personal testimony may be of help to us as we try to understand how God's gifts and calling work. His father, Charles E. Fuller, radio preacher for nearly forty years on the Old Fashioned Revival Hour and founder of Fuller Theological Seminary, surely was gifted by God to be an evangelist. One of his hopes was that his son would follow in his steps and continue the ministry as radio evangelist. Instead Dan Fuller became a teacher, Professor of Hermeneutics (biblical interpretation) at Fuller. The struggle he had with this decision is worth recounting.

When he became really interested in Christian things in his teens, his first thought was to be an evangelist, as his parents hoped he would. He shared this hope because, in the Christian culture in which he was raised, a teacher was viewed as low on the ladder. Those who could, did, Dan Fuller had been told, and those who could not, taught. Dan felt that teaching was the most undesirable of all the gifts and so tried very hard to be an evangelist.

But God never gave him much indication that this was his gift. Something like seven times, he took the 67 hour-long broadcast of the Old Fashioned Revival Hour. When it came time, with three or four minutes left on the air, he would give an invitation. Not one hand was raised in the great Long Beach Municipal Auditorium. This was a most distressing thing, because he never remembered his father's giving an altar call without getting a response.

Nevertheless, he persevered in trying to be an evangelist and worked actively on gospel teams in college campus evangelism. But even there, he was not able to find anyone who had been born again through his ministry.

Then, in the midst of these attempts at evangelism, he received a phone call from the dean at Fuller Theological Seminary, his Alma Mater. Upon graduation he had written a thesis on the Gospel of Mark. The dean said to him, "Dan, one of our professors has had a heart attack. He's teaching a course on the Gospel of Mark. He won't be able to complete the course. Will you take over?"

Dan Fuller did not really want to do it. He was wrapped up in college evangelism, but he said yes anyway. And then it happened: he was amazed at the contrast between the success of his teaching and the failure of his evangelism.

He learned that God gives gifts—not as we or our parents, or other people would will—but as he wills.

*Training for the Tasks of Leadership*

The gifts of God's Spirit do not work automatically. They work in and through our human personalities. We are persons, not robots. God has made us with great capability for growth. Almost anything we do, we do better with training.

## Gifts and Their Cultivation: Part One

In the early days of Christ's work, most of that training took place in the midst of the mission itself. John the Baptist took his students with him as he preached his words of repentance and prepared the way for the Messiah. Jesus did the same with his apostles, tutoring them intensively in the truths of God's kingdom before he sent them out on their own. And the apostle Paul followed that pattern with young persons like Mark and Timothy. Even at the beginning, training was essential.

Today we have schools to help with that training. But the principle is the same. Schools give us a steady and organized opportunity to study with God's people, to share their Christian experience, to learn from their knowledge, and to watch them at work.

Most Bible colleges and seminaries that provide training for leadership combine classroom studies with practical experience in evangelism and teaching. This is the ideal way to learn—studying and putting those studies to work.

*Study with good people* who know God's Word and put it to work in their lives—that is the first principle of training. In the minds and books of other Christian leaders there is the stuff of which the next generation of leaders is made.

The second principle is this: *get as much training as your opportunity and your ability allow.* It is difficult to get too much training, especially when we intend to work in countries like Canada and the United States where the educational level keeps rising. Here a word about patience may be helpful. In my own long years of graduate study, I was encouraged by Jesus' example: he spent thirty years preparing for a ministry which lasted three years.

Daniel Fuller has thoroughly understood the importance of training—both from his own experience and from the examples of hundreds of students whom he has taught.

Once he had decided that the Lord had given him the gift of teaching and that was to be his calling, he went on for further study. I shall let him tell why and how in his own words: "If you're going to be a teacher in a theological seminary, you just have to have an earned doctorate. And so I went off to a seminary in Chicago. My parents were not very happy about my prolonged absence, especially when I discovered that I had to spend even more time to learn the German language and be able to do research in German books and articles. So five years after getting a degree in Chicago, I felt led to go to Europe to master the German language and to sit under some of the leading theologians of this century.

"My parents were really upset when I took my wife and their four grandchildren 5,000 miles away to the University of Basel. I remember my mother saying, 'Dan, you won't be a bit better teacher by getting this training than you are already. Why are you tearing out our hearts by going off for a term of study that will be at least three years long?' But I felt definitely and unmistakably led by the Lord to take this training. And the benefits that it has had for me in teaching after returning home have been incalculable."

Formal training may end when we graduate from Bible school, college, or seminary. But actual training never ends. We continue to learn until the day we die. And then we shall understand God's truth as well as he has understood us (1 Corinthians 13:12)!

We learn best from the *example of effective leaders.* That is why younger pastors, teachers, and evangelists often associate themselves with more mature leaders for a number of years before they assume full leadership of a church or missionary enterprise.

We also learn from the *evaluation of sensitive believers*. As we practice our ministries, we cannot fully trust our own judgment regarding how we are doing. We need the wisdom of others who watch us as we work and who work with us. Their constructive suggestions can help us to do better. Especially can they encourage us in the areas where we are already doing well. Ministry is built on strengths, not weaknesses. The important thing for us to work on is the thing we do well. As we minister effectively, the Lord will bless our efforts and crown them with the success that only he can give.

Those of us who are teachers in schools or churches have a great deal of opportunity to let other members of the body of Christ help us develop our gifts. The questions and comments of my students over the years have driven me back to the Scriptures to study them from a new vantage point and learn things that I would never have learned without that stimulus. And, perhaps even more, students have taught me how to apply God's Word to my own life and to the life of the church. Their eagerness to learn and live God's Word has brought out the best in me time and again.

Deciding, training, practicing—those are the steps we take in preparing for Christian leadership. As we gain maturity through the work of God's Spirit, we can lead others into that maturity of life and character which Jesus desires for each of us. As his leaders, we minister to his ministers—like the 539 of them in our neighboring church. There is no finer task than this.

# 7

---

# Gifts and Their
# Cultivation: Part Two

*The end of all things is at hand; therefore keep sane and sober for your prayers. Above all hold unfailing your love for one another, since love covers a multitude of sins. Practice hospitality ungrudgingly to one another. As each has received a gift, employ it for one another, as good stewards of God's varied grace: whoever speaks, as one who utters oracles of God; whoever renders service, as one who renders it by the strength which God supplies; in order that in everything God may be glorified through Jesus Christ. To him belong glory and dominion for ever and ever. Amen.*

*1 Peter 4:7–11*

G ifted people often reserve the right to be temperamental. And the public usually supports that
right. Rock singers throw tantrums that destroy furni-
ture in their hotel suites and are rarely arrested. Star
baseball players throw dirt on umpires while 50,000
fans cheer them on. Movie actors flaunt their immoral
behavior, while their fawning public leers at the accounts in the gossip columns. The prima donna soprano
throws her fan at the conductor when he does not
let her shine long enough on the high 'C.'

Childish behavior—all of these examples—but ac-
cepted because giftedness and temperament are
thought to go hand in hand. Genius is supposed to
convey a free pass to selfishness.

None of this foolishness applies to God's people
who are gifted by his Spirit. That giftedness must express itself in discipline, not selfishness.

No part of Scripture makes this plainer than Peter's
words of wisdom to his young Christian friends: "The
end of all things is at hand; therefore keep sane and    75

sober for your prayers. Above all hold unfailing your love for one another, since love covers a multitude of sins. Practice hospitality ungrudgingly to one another. As each has received a gift, employ it for one another, as good stewards of God's varied grace: whoever speaks, as one who utters oracles of God; whoever renders service, as one who renders it by the strength which God supplies; in order that in everything God may be glorified through Jesus Christ. To him belong glory and dominion for ever and ever. Amen" (1 Peter 4:7–11).

*Gifts of stewardship* we can call this list, taking the cue from Peter's own phrase "good stewards of God's varied grace." That term, gifts of stewardship, reminds us that the gifts of hospitality, speaking, and service are powers that God entrusts to us so that we can do work for him. Things that he, as Master, does especially well—like welcoming us as members of his family, speaking to us with convincing power, and providing for our needs with supernatural strength—he now charges some of his people to do and gives special equipment so that they can do it. They are his good stewards drawing on grace he abundantly supplies. They have only one aim: to do the Master's bidding.

And that means doing his work in his way. Good stewards are different from glamorous stars. They are not laws unto themselves; they are bound to the Master's rules. Those rules insist that in whatever we do for him, we do with three great realities in mind: 1) the significance of love; 2) the importance of humility; 3) the centrality of Jesus Christ. Cultivating spiritual gifts takes more than training and practice at *doing;* it takes training and practice at *being.* Christian character is an essential part of Christian service. In God's

**76**

program no one is gifted enough for his churlishness to be acceptable. Neither generosity nor even martyrdom, the ultimate gift, count anything with God unless love is their motivation (1 Corinthians 13). God's gifts are like jewels whose beauty and brilliance are marred if their settings are tarnished and tinny.

*The Significance of Love*

Nothing demonstrates Christian truth so effectively as love. The reason for this is obvious: Christian truth is truth about God's love for us—love that he lavished upon Israel in the Old Testament, love that he displayed in sending his Son in the New Testament. Christian truth is also truth about God's power to change our lives—change our lives by replacing our selfishness with love.

Peter's *argument* for the significance of love was simple and direct: ". . . love covers a multitude of sins" (1 Peter 4:8). Of course, Peter did not mean that by our love we atone for our sins. Only Jesus' death could do that. What he clearly meant was that love does two things: it keeps us from being overcritical of other persons' faults, and it draws others to seek God's forgiveness. In both cases love helps to conquer sin.

Peter's *illustration* of the significance of love is the gift of hospitality—*entertaining the needy with grace.* In the early decades of the church, this gift was indispensable. Christian evangelists (we would call them missionaries) traveled frequently from city to city. There were almost no public lodging places available. What inns they may have found were little better than taverns or brothels, unsafe and corrupt. The growth and expansion of the church were enhanced by the    77 hospitality which believers extended to the traveling preachers.

Hospitality was an essential part of church life for another reason. New believers were frequently thrust out of their homes and cut off from their families. Without the food, shelter, and love of other Christians, their very lives were in jeopardy.

Peter viewed this hospitality as an attitude as well as an act. It could not be done well if it was done grudgingly. An open door must be matched by an open heart; warm bread tastes best when spread with a warm welcome. Nothing makes a guest more uncomfortable than to know that she is just being tolerated, not truly received. The same grace and generosity with which a loving heavenly Father has swung the door wide open and ushered us into the heart of his family circle must mark those who have the gift of hospitality. Act and attitude must be in harmony.

## The Importance of Humility

Giftedness and arrogance are arch-enemies—as hostile toward each other as giftedness and selfishness. Gift and pride do not belong in the same sentence.

Peter knew that and, therefore, urged his readers toward humility with words like these: ". . . whoever renders service, as one who renders it by the strength which God supplies" (1 Peter 4:11). That last line slams the door on pride—what we do as Christians in service to others we do in "the strength which God supplies."

Humility is important for a number of reasons. First, our ability to render significant service is a *gift*, not an achievement. Good service takes selflessness; it means setting aside what we might prefer to do to give attention to the needs of others. Jesus illustrates this gift, with the towel and basin, when he washes his disciples' feet (John 13:1–20). Such serving does not come naturally to us. We would rather be waited on than to wait on others.

Humility is important for a second reason: service is not only a gift; it is a *gift of God*. This makes it both precious and purposeful. The value of a gift is partly due to the giver. Special friends or important persons convey a preciousness to any gift they give beyond its monetary worth. What are gifts from God worth? His honor, glory, and dignity place them beyond price, even though on the face of it they may seem menial—like washing someone's feet.

The gift of service is purposeful as well as precious. Its purpose is powerfully stated by Peter: ". . . in order that in everything God may be glorified through Jesus Christ" (1 Peter 4:11). Washing feet, cleaning house, doing shopping, cooking food, bringing flowers—all to the glory of God! Daily chores that we do for the helpless and regular tasks that we perform in the church have the highest possible dignity because they make God's glory known and bring joy to his heart.

This purpose is specifically stated, because it is such an overwhelming temptation for me to take credit for the service I render. After all, I saw the opportunity and chose to help. And I have a certain amount of personal strength that I can bring to the task, or so I reason.

Spiritually, that is bad thinking. I take credit for what I do and it becomes easy then for me to look down on the person whom I serve. Service becomes *my* work, not *God's*. *My* purposes get served—pride, self-satisfaction, public acclaim—not *God's*. All of life goes out of kilter, and the service becomes a liability to the church instead of an asset. Whatever polishes **79** human glory tarnishes God's glory. To let that happen is an unspeakable mistake. Cultivating God's spiritual gifts calls us to honor the importance of humility in all we do or, to put it better, in all he does through us.

## The Centrality of Jesus Christ

In music, the arts, athletics, or politics, it is customary for gifted people to call attention to themselves. Actors treasure their curtain calls; artists revel in their exhibitions; athletes hoard their newspaper clippings; politicians puff up when their admirers make glowing speeches about them.

God's gifted people—and that is all of us—should work from motivations different from those. It is the honor of Christ that we seek. The applause must go to him.

This is especially true in the exercise of the gift of speaking. As stewards of God's grace, as servants doing his work in his power, we cannot preach a message of our choosing. Whoever speaks, Peter instructed, should speak "as one who utters oracles of God" (1 Peter 4:11). What are these oracles? The promises and requirements of the living God who has made himself known to us in Jesus his Son.

This side of Bethlehem's stable, Golgotha's cross, and Jerusalem's empty tomb, God's oracles are about Jesus. He is God's final word to us. Our speaking, then, in the Spirit's power must center in Jesus' words and deeds. His lordship is what we proclaim; his glory is what we covet: "in order that in everything God may be glorified through Jesus Christ. To him belong glory and dominion for ever and ever. Amen" (1 Peter 4:11).

Not our pet persuasions, not our private hunches, not our own religious aspirations—but Jesus Christ to whom all glory and dominion belong is the theme of our preaching and teaching when we do it in the power of the Spirit. To cultivate the gifts of the Spirit we focus on Jesus. After all, the reason God sent his Spirit was to make Jesus known.

Entertaining with grace, serving with dependence, and speaking of Christ with assurance—these are the gifts of stewardship. They are to be performed not just with skill, but with poise and gracefulness. The *how* of our stewardship is just as important as the *what.* The significance of love, the importance of humility, and the centrality of Jesus Christ—without these, whatever gifts we try to cultivate will rot before they ripen. And Christ's church will suffer from malnutrition.

These spiritual emphases apply, of course, not only to Peter's list of the gifts of stewardship, but to all the other gifts as well. Paul blazoned *the significance of love* before the eyes of the Christians at Corinth. They were caught up in competition. Using the Spirit's gifts of power, they struggled with each other to demonstrate their importance. Their services must have looked more like the Olympic contests than the Christian community. The great love chapter (1 Corinthians 13) was Paul's rebuke of their lovelessness. Gifts of tongues or prophecy or faith without love are nothing. That was how strongly Paul expressed himself.

*The importance of humility* Paul spotlighted in the gifts of service: ". . . I bid every one among you not to think of himself more highly than he ought to think" (Romans 12:3). Making financial contributions, rendering mercy, giving aid—these may be done in our own strength. But when they are, they are not gifts of the Spirit. Work done in his power must only humble us, not puff us up.

*The centrality of Jesus Christ* must be maintained     81

whatever gift we have and use. This is preeminently true in the gifts of leadership (Ephesians 4). Evangelists and pastor-teachers fail miserably unless Jesus is the center of their ministry. After all, their task is to lead people ". . . to mature manhood, to the measure of the stature of the fulness of Christ" (Ephesians 4:13). How can that possibly be done if human personality and human thinking are our message?

If the world wants to celebrate temperamental stars, so be it. The church can have no part of that. Stewardship calls for another way of life. There the work is done on the Master's orders, with attitudes pleasing to him. He supplies the power; that is his task. We give him the credit; that is our privilege.

# 8

## Gifts and the Tragedy of Neglect

"For it will be as when a man going on a journey called his
servants and entrusted to them his property; to one he gave
five talents, to another two, to another one, to each according
to his ability. Then he went away. He who had received the
five talents went at once and traded with them; and he made
five talents more. So also, he who had the two talents made
two talents more. But he who had received the one talent went
and dug in the ground and hid his master's money. Now after
a long time the master of those servants came and settled
accounts with them. And he who had received the five talents
came forward, bringing five talents more, saying, 'Master, you
delivered to me five talents; here I have made five talents more.'
His master said to him, 'Well done, good and faithful servant;
you have been faithful over a little, I will set you over much;
enter into the joy of your master.' And he also who had the
two talents came forward, saying, 'Master, you delivered to me
two talents; here I have made two talents more.' His master
said to him, 'Well done, good and faithful servant; you have
been faithful over a little, I will set you over much; enter into
the joy of your master.' He also who had received the one talent
came forward, saying, 'Master, I knew you to be a hard man,
reaping where you did not sow, and gathering where you did
not winnow; so I was afraid, and I went and hid your talent
in the ground. Here you have what is yours.' But his master
answered him, 'You wicked and slothful servant! You knew
that I reap where I have not sowed, and gather where I have
not winnowed? Then you ought to have invested my money
with the bankers, and at my coming I should have received
what was my own with interest. So take the talent from him,
and give it to him who has the ten talents. For to every one
who has will more be given, and he will have abundance; but
from him who has not, even what he has will be taken away.
And cast the worthless servant into the outer darkness; there
men will weep and gnash their teeth."
Matthew 25:14–30

What's wrong with the church today? That question is raised in a hundred different ways and by as many voices.

And for every form of the question there is more than one possible answer. There are many things wrong with the church today, just as there have been many things wrong with it throughout the centuries since Jesus came to establish it.

Name your problem, and you can find some form of it among the congregations and denominations that make up Christ's body on earth. In some places the churches are not true to the teaching of the Scriptures. They have imposed their own views of God's program, will, and nature on the Bible. They pick and choose the parts they want to believe and cast aside the others.

In other places, the churches have lost their vision for mission and evangelism. All their energies are expended in caring for their own members; their horizons reach only to the back pews of their own buildings. They behave as though Jesus had died only for them, 85 or as though men and women were all going to heaven regardless of what they believed.

Many things are wrong with the church! Divisions that stem from bigotry, heresies that grow out of biblical ignorance, personality cults that celebrate human achievement, compromise with pagan values in sexual and marital matters—all these give the church a clinical rating that ranks with some of the sickest persons in an intensive care ward.

Yet nothing debilitates the church and weakens its mission more than the neglect of spiritual gifts. The situation in thousands of congregations is literally tragic.

And all of this despite Jesus' strong warning. One of his best known stories speaks specifically to the tragedy that God's people suffer when they do not make the most of the gifts that God has given them. The story is the Parable of the Talents whose familiar themes are found in Matthew 25:14–30. Three tragedies come to light in the course of that parable. They describe our present problems with the accuracy of tomorrow's headlines: 1) the tragedy of abused accountability; 2) the tragedy of missed opportunity; 3) the tragedy of lost joy. Let us walk through the story, survey these three tragedies, and see what we can do to avoid them. No account of the discovery and cultivation of our spiritual gifts can be complete, if we fail to note the damage done when those gifts are neglected.

*The Tragedy of Abused Accountability*

The people in the parable are one key to its message: a master and three servants. That relationship speaks of accountability. Servants must answer to their masters in all details of their life and work. We make a great mistake when we mix our role with God's. He sets the terms of our work. He is in all things the Master; our task is not to make the rules, but to say "yes" to the rules he has already made.

*We are accountable to the Master's grace.* Remember how Jesus began his parable: "For it will be as when a man going on a journey called his servants and entrusted to them his property; to one he gave five talents, to another two, to another one, to each according to his ability. Then he went away" (Matthew 25:14–15).

Who decided who would get the five, the two, and the one? The Master, of course. Only he knew the servants well enough to determine how much property each of them had ability to handle. There was no squabble among them, no elbowing each other for the largest share, no badgering the Master for an extra talent. They recognized his right to decide. They had no property of their own, nor any power to acquire it. Their share was determined by his grace, and by that grace alone.

It was that grace that held them accountable. It placed them under obligation to make the best possible response. What they had not earned or deserved had been put in their trust; their only acceptable answer was to use it well.

So it is with the gifts of God's Spirit. The Master of the church gives them as expressions of his grace. We do not choose which gifts or how many. Those matters are up to him. Most important, we cannot choose not to use what he has given us—not without abusing our accountability to his grace.

*We are accountable to the Master's purpose*—the purpose for which he lavished his grace upon us. This fact is made clear in the master's rebuke of the servant    87 who hid his one talent: "You wicked and slothful servant! You knew that I reap where I have not sowed, and gather where I have not winnowed. Then you ought to have invested my money with the bankers, and at my coming I should have received what was my own with interest" (Matthew 25:26–27). The word *interest* catches our eye. It tells us that God's grace in our lives is counted as an investment. It is not just to be conserved. That was the wretched servant's mistake. He did not realize that grace is a seed to be planted for further growth. He did not understand that God's blessings are not for hoarding, but for multiplying as we put them to work in the lives of others.

That servant could not plead ignorance. He knew precisely how demanding the master was. But he misapplied the knowledge that he had. He was defensive, not aggressive. He took no risks in using the master's grace and, in so doing, took the greatest risk of all: he neglected his accountability to the master's purpose.

The gifts of God's Holy Spirit are precious and true. And the Lord of the church demandingly wants them treated as such. But they are not like gold to be stored in Fort Knox nor like Rembrandt's paintings to be hung in a well-guarded museum. They are fuel to be converted into spiritual power; they are seedlings which will grow into fruitful trees; they are ore to be refined into useful tools. Any less profitable use of them will find the Master calling us to account.

### The Tragedy of Missed Opportunity

The fearful, cautious servant teaches us another lesson about God's grace: more is given when we use well what we have. Part of that servant's tragedy was that he missed his opportunity for greater blessing.

## Gifts and the Tragedy of Neglect

The master's command was harsh: "So take the talent from him, and give it to him who has the ten talents. For to every one who has will more be given, and he will have abundance; but from him who has not, even what he has will be taken away" (Matthew 25:28–29).

The greater responsibility, the larger privilege, the expanded service, the enhanced growth—all of these opportunities were missed because the servant misread his master's instructions. Even more tragically, he lost the one opportunity he had: his single talent had to be forfeited.

Who dares take lightly any gift of God after reading this story? We have Jesus' own word on it—unused gifts may lead to disqualification from God's service.

What would an athletic coach do in a situation like this? For weeks the coach has worked with a player to teach him one thing—to kick the extra points after touchdown for the football team. Patiently the coach has corrected the player's form and timing; cheerfully the coach has tried to bolster the kicker's confidence in his ability to boot the ball between the uprights and over the cross bar. Then came the game. The other team scored first, missed its extra point, and led 6–0 until the last minute. Finally our coach's team muscled over a touchdown and the stage was set for the well-drilled kicker to enter the game. The line blocked, the ball was snapped, the holder set it down, but, to the dismay of team, fans, and coach, the kicker snatched the ball and fell on it. He had kept it from the other team; the ball was safe. But he had failed in the single duty for which he had been so meticulously prepared, and his team did not win.

Will the coach give him further responsibility? Will he reward him for his cautious, conservative play? Of course not. The coach's goal was to win. All his loving attention was for that purpose. The aim of his grace was to lead his team to victory. The kicker missed that aim completely.

The tragedy that has crippled so many churches and turned their members into losers is that the Spirit's gifts have not been put to work for God's purposes. And the God of all grace has seen fit to withdraw that grace from them and pour it out elsewhere.

## The Tragedy of Lost Joy

The story of the talents is tragedy—not comedy— in its form. Its focus is more on losing than winning. Its climax is the condemnation of the one unfaithful servant rather than the commendation of the two good ones. This parable is a warning of the tragedy of abused accountability and missed opportunity. It is also a tragedy of lost joy, and this may be its most pathetic note.

The pathos comes in the contrast between the master's blessing of the two obedient servants and his dismissal of the wicked servant. To those who invested his grace to multiply it he spoke these words of affirmation: "Well done, good and faithful servant; you have been faithful over a little, I will set you over much; enter into the joy of your master" (Matthew 25:21,23). To the other servant his command was hopelessly grim: "And cast the worthless servant into the outer darkness; there men will weep and gnash their teeth" (Matthew 25:30).

No word here about the joy of the master. At the very least that final sentence means exclusion from the fellowship of God's people and the blessings of his grace. The master had hoped for better things. He longed to bless and reward *all* his servants. His joy was to get his work done and to see his people do it well.

But no joy is available in that outer darkness. *No joy for the servant.* He was accountable to his lord, and he abused that accountability; he had been granted a magnificent opportunity to please his master and he missed that opportunity. Only chagrin and regret could have been his emotions.

The lesson of this parable leaps at us from the page: no church, no Christian dares neglect the spiritual gifts which God's grace has bestowed for God's joy.

But what are our churches doing? We know that something is often wrong with them, but what can we do to set right that wrong?

Dr. Roberta Hestenes is a professor at Fuller Theological Seminary and a Presbyterian minister. She has had wide experience in helping churches strengthen their ministries by putting their spiritual gifts to work. Here are some of her comments on what churches need to do and are doing.

"I am very encouraged by much of the recent emphasis in our congregations on the discovery of spiritual gifts—the good news that God has gifted all of the members of his body, that each one has been given a ministry to exercise in the empowerment of the Holy Spirit. And I am also glad for the rediscovery of the fact that our congregations should be contexts within which spiritual gifts can be discovered and exercised. Sometimes I am discouraged to find that people do not understand that ministry belongs to all of the family of God, that everyone has been gifted, whether clergy or lay person.

"But there is a lot that is encouraging in this particular area. It's encouraging to discover that God has gifted women as well as men, that he has gifted the laity    91 as well as clergy, that every person has a place in God's plan.

"I have found that spiritual gifts are not discovered by looking in the mirror, but rather are discovered in the context of a Christian congregation in which we experience support and a chance to exercise ministry. Here is a sample list of persons whose ministries I have watched with joyful appreciation.

. . . Rae, a woman in our congregation, used to feel that she did not have much to contribute but has found in recent years that she had a significant ministry in providing meals for the elderly. Day by day she is carrying food to people in need.

. . . Bob has discovered that sponsoring sack lunches in his engineering firm has encouraged discussions about ethics and the will of God that have been very helpful to the persons with whom he works.

. . . Jim works with a Boy Scout troop. By helping those boys build kayaks, he is building them in their character and is a witness to them of what the love of Christ looks like in action.

. . . A woman has gone door to door in her neighborhood for the first time in her life, asking her neighbors if they would like to come to a neighborhood Bible study. And she has started to share the Good News by leading them through a discussion about the Gospel of Mark.

"All this evidence that spiritual gifts are being put to use ought to be of great encouragement to the pastors in our churches. For them, I think of the words from Exodus 18 in which Jethro said to Moses: 'Why do you labor alone and do all of this work? This is not good. God has given you people to help to carry the burden and to share in the ministry.' And I believe that in our congregations God has gifted people so they may do the ministry God wants to accomplish. Our task as pastors is to release people for ministry, to encourage them, to train them, to equip them."

Roberta Hestenes' description of the work of God's people reminds us that tragedy need not be the final word. God's Spirit has enabled hundreds of churches to turn tragedy to triumph when his people come to grips with what he has granted them grace to accomplish. The investment of spiritual gifts can pay dividends that will rescue churches from spiritual bankruptcy. By discovering your gift and putting it to work you can be part of that rescue.

# 9

---

# Gifts Unmentioned in the Bible

*So when they had come together, they asked him, "Lord, will you at this time restore the kingdom to Israel?" He said to them, "It is not for you to know times or seasons which the Father has fixed by his own authority. But you shall receive power when the Holy Spirit has come upon you; and you shall be my witnesses in Jerusalem and in all Judea and Samaria and to the end of the earth." And when he had said this, as they were looking on, he was lifted up, and a cloud took him out of their sight. And while they were gazing into heaven as he went, behold, two men stood by them in white robes, and said, "Men of Galilee, why do you stand looking into heaven? This Jesus, who was taken up from you into heaven, will come in the same way as you saw him go into heaven."*

*Acts 1:6–11*

The sound of it still sends shivers down my back. The rich timbre of that voice, its ringing resonance, its compassionate urgency compelled millions of people to heed the claims of God and to rejoice in his grace. Radio has heard nothing like it since Charles E. Fuller died in 1968.

His voice was a thing apart, whether asking "Honey" to go right ahead with the letters, lifting the congregation to the strains of "Heavenly Sunshine," singing "Meet Me There" in camp meeting fashion, or inviting the war-time sailors to come to Christ in the Long Beach Municipal Auditorium. Even the tapes of Dr. Fuller's broadcasts, which are still played on some Christian radio stations, can recreate the spiritual power of his presence and concern as he expressed it through his voice.

I have no doubt that God's Spirit used that voice in an uncommon way to herald the gospel on more than 800 stations worldwide in the dark days of depression and war. Charles E. Fuller's voice, a landmark for nearly forty years of broadcasting on the Old Fashioned Revival Hour, is an example of a spiritual gift which the Bible does not mention.

How many gifts like this there are, no one knows. The best we can do is to list a few and point the way toward some others. What we do know is that God's Spirit has freedom to work the way he wills. And we must be open to his work—and to his surprises, as Paul seemed to be in adding the gifts of philanthropy and martyrdom to the list that he had spelled out so systematically in 1 Corinthians 12:4–11 (see 1 Corinthians 13:3).

How the Holy Spirit works and what we need to do—those are the two important matters for us to look at in this study. We do not want to miss what God has for us or to neglect what he has given us. We may not all have that urging, inviting, convicting voice of a great radio evangelist, but each of us has a gift. If we have not yet discovered that gift in the four great New Testament lists—gifts of service (Romans 12), gifts of power (1 Corinthians 12), gifts of leadership (Ephesians 4), gifts of stewardship (1 Peter 4)— then we must keep trying. Finding our place of service in God's program is as important as anything else we can do.

*How the Holy Spirit Works*

To understand the ministry of God's Holy Spirit, we need to go back to Jesus' announcement of the Spirit's coming. The setting was the forty-day period between Jesus' resurrection and his ascension. He was preparing his disciples for their role in his kingdom, a kingdom whose nature they did not yet understand. The Book of Acts describes their question about it:

"So when they had come together, they asked him, 'Lord, will you at this time restore the kingdom to Israel?' He said to them, 'It is not for you to know times or seasons which the Father has fixed by his own authority. But you shall receive power when the Holy Spirit has come upon you; and you shall be my witnesses in Jerusalem and in all Judea and Samaria and to the end of the earth' " (Acts 1:6–8).

*The real gift of God is the Spirit.* That was Jesus' first point. The disciples were asking a political question about Israel's future. Would God's chosen people again have their own political sovereignty? Would Jesus, as David's son, set up a throne, snatch the scepter from Roman hands, and usher in the new age of political and religious freedom?

Jesus' answer both turned the questions aside and gave them a profound reply. The eye was not to be on history's calendar, but on the coming of the Spirit. In the person of the Spirit, the power and glory of God's kingdom would be present. And the Spirit would enable them to be effective servants of that kingdom.

Jesus wasted no effort spelling out the details of the Spirit's work. He pinpointed instead the Spirit's power and presence in the church. God himself has come to work in us—that is what the Spirit's coming means. He is the real gift of God. When we have him we have God's full equipment to do our part of the work in his kingdom.

*The Spirit's presence gives us power.* That was Jesus' second point: "But you shall receive power when the Holy Spirit has come upon you." Throughout the Bible, the Holy Spirit is connected with divine power. As the winds impel the clouds and drive them to their destination where they drop their welcome rain, so the Spirit—the wind of God—empowers the people of God to serve his purposes. As God breathed into the red clay of Eden and saw Adam spring to life, so he sends his Spirit—the divine breath—to bring life to his church.

All of God's people, people who have committed their lives to Jesus Christ as their Lord and Savior, have this power. That is why we can serve as witnesses—as testifiers, givers of firsthand evidence—to the saving grace that has come to us in Jesus. The Spirit gives our lives consistency so that what we say is supported by how we live; the Spirit gives our hearts courage so that we can bear witness to God's work even under threat of persecution; the Spirit gives our words conviction so that others will take seriously what we say about Jesus. His holy presence within his people gives us power.

*The Spirit's power works everywhere and in all kinds of ways.* Think of how Jesus' promise has been fulfilled in the centuries since the Day of Pentecost when the Spirit was sent to the church by God the Father and God the Son. The witnesses of Jesus' power to save have moved out into every nation so that today there is scarcely a spot of any size on a map of the inhabited world where there is not a Christian congregation worshiping God in Jesus' name.

Think what it took to bring that about. Christian missionaries spent their lives learning languages, understanding cultures, mastering foreign customs in order to tell people about Jesus. Christian merchants travelled from place to place not only buying and selling, but also sharing their experience of salvation through Jesus. Christian monks established monasteries, taught their trades to their neighbors, and witnessed to Jesus' love by the discipline and holiness of their dedicated lives. Christian martyrs (the literal meaning of that word is *witnesses*) demonstrated the power of their faith by laying down their lives for it. From their blood the church absorbed new life.

Missionaries, merchants, monks, martyrs—these and a vast army of ordinary people like you and me—spread the Word, lived the life, sang the song of salvation, and planted the church. What a host of spiritual gifts were at work to dot the pages of church history with its exciting stories of growth! The great gift—God's own Spirit—was, and is yet, equipping his people to make his kingship known. That great gift brought into play dozens of special gifts that made spiritual success possible in a world of religious ignorance and moral uncleanness. That is how the Spirit works.

*What We Need to Do*

How does each of us fit in the Spirit's program to tell others who Jesus is and what he has done? Which of the variety of his gifts do I have? What if I have combed through the lists in the New Testament and have not found a gift that seems to describe what I can do? Discovering the answer to those hard questions takes time and patience. Here are some steps that may help.

First, *believe that you have a spiritual gift.* Doubt about this can trap you into discouragement. One of the devil's meanest tricks is to try to handicap God's team by keeping some of the players on the bench or in the grandstands. Christ's ministry must be carried on by every part of his body; he wants no idle members; his Spirit is resident within each member with a gift for ministry. Believe that *you* have one of those gifts.

The second step is this: *watch other Christians at work.* From the way God uses them you can catch ideas about your own ministry. Some gifts are quite obvious, like Charles Fuller's awesome voice, or the musical sensitivity of Rudy Atwood, for years the pianist on the Old Fashioned Revival Hour and The Joyful Sound. Speaking of music, more than mere talent is needed for it to be called a spiritual gift. Talent may impress or even dazzle. The gift of music ministers. Through it the Spirit takes words and music and uses them to move the human heart to trust in God. George Beverly Shea has that gift; so do many other dedicated soloists.

If you do not have an obvious gift like music, keep looking. Some persons have a gift for learning languages and do very well at Bible study and translation or at ministering to people of other cultures.

*Listening* to other persons with patience, understanding, and compassion can be a gift. George Doyal is my wife's nephew. He has been a missionary to Japan. Since he was a young boy he has had the unusual ability to listen to others, especially people from foreign countries. The Lord used this gift to help call him to his several ministries, first in Tokyo, where he worked with university students, then in Pasadena where he serves in an agency that sends Christians to teach English in China.

Counseling takes just this kind of listening with the wisdom to help people apply God's truths—especially the truths of his love and grace—to their lives. My friend Joan has that gift. God uses her warm patience and sensitive understanding almost every day to help others. And all along she has raised a family, cared for a husband, and ministered to an aged parent.

**102**      Problem-solving may also be a spiritual gift. Carl

George, for instance, the director of the Charles E. Fuller Institute for Evangelism and Church Growth has that gift. The Lord has given him unusual insight into the problems that various denominations and congregations need to solve if they are going to grow in numbers and in spirit.

These are just a few examples to illustrate my point. Watching people like these exercise their gifts can help each of us know what we are good at and how we can serve in Christ's ministry.

That brings us to the third step: *Do what you enjoy.* The gifts of the Spirit and the joy of the Spirit usually go hand in hand.

No one who ever saw Charles Fuller in a pulpit or Rudy Atwood at a piano could doubt that. What God had made them good at they enjoyed doing.

God wants you to be the same. What you enjoy in Christian work—teaching, counseling, listening, serving, planning, problem solving, offering hospitality—try and keep trying. If others of God's people respond to your work and enjoy it with you, that is an excellent indication that God has gifted you for that kind of work.

You have God's Spirit, and that Spirit wants to show Christ's love and power through your life. *Be open to the Spirit's direction.* That is the final step. He knows you, he loves you, he lives within you, he will work through you. How is up to him.

More than sixty years ago the Lord took a shy, burly orange rancher and equipped him to speak to the nations through the wonder of radio. No one was more surprised by the effectiveness of his ministry than Charles Fuller. The Spirit of God is so full of such surprises that no one can guess where he will work next. Perhaps it will be in your life.

# 10

## Gifts and Talents and Genes

*For thou didst form my inward parts,*
 *thou didst knit me together in my mother's womb.*
*I praise thee, for thou art fearful and wonderful.*
 *Wonderful are thy works!*
*Thou knowest me right well;*
 *my frame was not hidden from thee,*
*when I was being made in secret,*
 *intricately wrought in the depths of the earth.*
*Thy eyes beheld my unformed substance;*
 *in thy book were written, every one of them,*
*the days that were formed for me,*
 *when as yet there was none of them.*
*How precious to me are thy thoughts, O God!*
 *How vast is the sum of them!*
*If I would count them, they are more than the sand.*
 *When I awake, I am still with thee.*
                              *Psalm 139:13–18*

A double mystery we can call it. Either half of it is puzzling enough by itself. Combined, the two halves defy solving.

The mystery is the way God's Spirit works through human personality. Both sides of that mystery are complicated beyond words.

Human personality is an incredible mix of tissue and spirit, of heredity and environment, of genes and training, of instincts and thoughts. How it works is something that gives thousands of psychologists attacks of insomnia.

And our theologians probably sleep even less as they ponder the wondrous ways in which God's Spirit works. Jesus baffled Nicodemus with his description of the mystery of the Spirit: "The wind blows where it wills, and you hear the sound of it, but you do not know whence it comes or whither it goes; so it is with every one who is born of the Spirit" (John 3:8). This comparison between the blowing of the wind and the work of God's Spirit may help us live with 107 our double mystery, even though it does not help us solve it.

Jesus warned Nicodemus and us against trying to figure out just how the Holy Spirit carries on his business. We can tell that he is at work not only by the results—like the sound of the wind rustling leaves in the tree tops—but the way in which he works is beyond our human ken. We can see the *what*, as lives are changed, as persons are encouraged, as the people of God mature in character and grow in number; but we cannot know the *how*.

This double mystery—God working through human beings—is nothing new. Israel's psalmists grappled with it ages ago:

> For thou didst form my inward parts,
>    thou didst knit me together in my
>    mother's womb.
> I praise thee, for thou art fearful
>    and wonderful.
>    Wonderful are thy works!
> Thou knowest me right well; my frame
>    was not hidden from
>    thee,
> When I was being made in secret, in-
>    tricately wrought in the depths
>    of the earth.
> Thy eyes beheld my unformed substance;
>    in thy book were written, every
>    one of them,
> the days that were formed for me,
>    when as yet there was none of
>    them.
> How precious to me are thy thoughts,
>    O God!
> How vast is the sum of them!

If I would count them, they are more
than the sand.
When I awake, I am still with
thee (Psalm 139:13–18).

Before we look more specifically at what the psalm
is teaching us, it might be well to remind ourselves
of what our question is. We are trying to gain some
light on the manifold ways in which God works
through us. What are we? We are a combination of
our genes, our training, and our spiritual gifts. As we
do God's will, all of these work together in the mystery
of God's grace. What is God? He is our Creator, our
Lord, and our Enabler. All of these relationships work
in us simultaneously.

We must not, therefore, think of ourselves in terms
that are too compartmentalized, and we must not try
to tune too finely the various relationships that God
sustains to us. Perhaps we can begin to gain some light
on our double mystery of how God works through
us as we turn back to Psalm 139 and look at it in
some detail. We shall make some significant progress
if we can catch three basic lessons from the psalm:
1) a sense of *continuity* in the way God works; 2) a
sense of *confidence* in the results of God's work; 3) a
sense of *commitment* to share in God's work.

*A Sense of Continuity in the Way God Works*

"Hear, O Israel: The Lord our God is one Lord"
(Deuteronomy 6:4). Those words were drilled into the
hearts and minds of every son and daughter in Israel.
They were absorbed three times a day with the regular-
ity of meals, until they became part of the muscle
and marrow of each member of God's ancient family. **109**

The neighboring peoples that touched Israel's borders were all polytheists; each worshiped a cluster of divine beings, among whom were divided the responsibilities for the control of life. Storm gods, wind gods, fertility gods, gods of crops, of healing, of good fortune—all of these and more were part of the ancient pantheons, the company of gods to whom the Canaanites, Babylonians, and Egyptians looked for help.

Into this confused and divided religious scene Israel's Lord, Yahweh, came with his magnificent claim. All of life—creation, history, personal circumstances—was under his control. He was Lord everywhere and always and of everyone. Gladly the Israelites acknowledged his oneness, his exclusiveness: "The Lord our God is one Lord." One—not many. That reality brought a sense of continuity to their understanding of how God worked. From their understanding we can sharpen ours.

*He is Lord of our heredity.* "For thou didst form my inward parts, thou didst knit me together in my mother's womb" (Psalm 139:13). Conception, pregnancy, birth are not just natural happenstance—a lucky combination of sperm and ovum. God is at work in our lives from the beginning. We are not just the fruit of human reproduction; we are also the products of divine providence. God's attention to us begins long before we are interested in him. He plans far ahead for our place in his program, even before we are born. What, therefore, we have inherited from our parents— our looks, our energy level, our innate intelligence— are all part of what God wants us to be. They are the foundations on which he will build his plan for our lives. "The Lord our God is one Lord"; he is Lord of our heredity.

110    *He is Lord of our environment as well.* "Thy eyes

beheld my unformed substance; in thy book were written, every one of them, the days that were formed for me, when as yet there was none of them" (Psalm 139:16).

Talk about planning—the very days of our lives are written down by God before they happen. That was the psalmist's dramatic way of saying that God is in control of our circumstances. His lordship has a lot to do with the training we receive, the experiences we undergo, the setting in which we make our daily decisions. Of course, he is not responsible for our sin, our selfishness, or our disobedience. But he uses the environment in which we grow up to fit us for his service. "The Lord our God is one Lord"; he is Lord of our heredity and our environment.

*He is also Lord of our spiritual equipment.* The gifts that he bestows, the special abilities or powers that he gives us, work in harmony with his other provisions in our genes and our training. The gift of musical ministry, for instance, is usually based on some natural talents like a good ear for pitch or fine vocal apparatus. The gift of teaching may be given to those who have better than average intelligence or unusually retentive memories. The gift of hospitality may tie in with special training that was available in a home where the parents made it a practice to entertain others. "The Lord our God is one Lord"; he is Lord of our heredity, our environment, and our spiritual equipment.

I hope the point is clear. There is a continuity to the way God works in our lives. His is the initiative; the one personal Lord shaped my frame, chose my family, and gave me his Spirit with his special gifts. Mine is the involvement in that work; as a person I am not a series of compartments, but a subtle combination of the various ways in which God has worked. **111**

My particular parents with their energy, intelligence, and looks; my home with its Christian attitude, confidence in prayer, and attention to the Bible; my brothers and sister, with their ability in speech, sense of humor, and Christian commitment; my special training in languages and history; my combination of experiences in a small church where I was allowed to exercise responsibilities in leadership and in industry where I learned about organizational practices and working with people; and my particular spiritual gifts in teaching and administration—all of these combine to enable me to minister in Christ's name. And the one Lord is responsible for them all. His lordship gives a sense of continuity to the many ways in which he works.

*A Sense of Confidence in the Results of God's Work*

The marvel and mystery of God's ways in his life had our psalmist wide-eyed with amazement. He had *full confidence in God's sovereign power:* "I praise thee, for thou art fearful and wonderful. Wonderful are thy works!" (Psalm 139:14). And why not such praise? If God can fashion unique human persons capable of loving him and serving others from a couple of dots of living tissue, what can he not do? A knowledge of the many and varied facets of his providence sets us free to trust him, to believe that he will work— even through us.

The psalmist also had *full confidence in God's personal knowledge:* "How precious to me are thy thoughts, O God! How vast is the sum of them!" (Psalm 139:17). And why not such exclamation? God knows the plan of our days before they ever happen. When we did not have him in mind at all, he was already cherishing us and reserving for us a place in his plan. That is

112

thoughtfulness at its highest. Small wonder that we can count on him to carry out his mission—and to use us in it.

Doubt, discouragement, self-depreciation—these are worldly, not biblical, attitudes. We can always wish we were different or better. And there is ample room for improvement among even the best of God's people. But we must not disparage God's handiwork. That remarkable set of natural and spiritual abilities that combine in us are his doing. And he does all things well.

*A Sense of Commitment to Share in God's Work*

God does his work well, and he wants us to do ours the same way. There are some specific steps we can take as we seek to cooperate in God's plan for his people.

First, *we can accept ourselves as God's servants.* We are God's workmanship created and guided by him and recreated in Jesus Christ to do his good works. We are not proud of our failings, and we are downright ashamed of our sinning. But we must not reject ourselves; we must not brand ourselves as worthless; we must not disqualify ourselves from God's service. If we do, we insult our Creator, Provider, and Enabler. We slap God in the face and tell him that he does not know what he is doing. We may not understand the mysteries of how God has shaped our lives, but we must not doubt that he has shaped them. There are purposes that he has prepared us to fulfill; we can accept ourselves and get on with those purposes.

Second, *we can offer ourselves to God's service.* We may continue to ponder those twin mysteries of how God works and how we fit. But we do not wait for **113** their answer before we go to work. We place our lives before God and say, "Whatever I am, whatever you have made me, I offer to you. Here I am. Send me. Speak, Lord, for your servant hears."

Finally, *we can give God the credit for our service.* Our genes, our talents, our training, our spiritual gifts—each of them, all of them, we take from God's own hand. What we are able to do in his work with any of these gifts is really God's work. The honor, the glory, the recognition must be his. No service can be of full significance if we keep hogging the credit. Any service is of eternal weight if God gains the honor through it.

So, we let the mystery be what it is. We cannot get our tiny minds around God's ways; we cannot fathom the depths of our own personalities. But we can accept ourselves before God, offer ourselves to his purposes, and pledge ourselves to see that the glory is his.

# 11

## Gifts and the Spirit's Fruit

*But the fruit of the Spirit is love, joy, peace, patience, kindness, goodness, faithfulness, gentleness, self-control; against such there is no law. And those who belong to Christ Jesus have crucified the flesh with its passions and desires.*
*Galatians 5:22–24*

What is the key to the success of the Los Angeles Dodgers? Teamwork. At least that is the answer given in a radio commercial familiar to thousands of Dodger fans.

Teamwork may have helped the baseball players win the National League pennant in far more than their share of years. But it is no secret to those who follow baseball closely that the famous teamwork has exploded into dissension on several occasions. Two stars fought in the locker room before a game a few years ago. Another star called one of the Dodger presidents a liar in a dispute over whether the star had been promised that he would receive the second highest salary on the team.

Spirited American men, we call them. They are proud, highstrung, competitive achievers, with a high sense of honor as to how they are treated. For them achievement and pride go hand in hand. Their coaches, teammates and fans tolerate all kinds of surly, peevish, abusive, or explosive behavior from players who are valuable to the team. And, of course, the sportswriters thrive on the stories of irrational or unseemly behavior.

As long as the pitcher can hold the other team to two runs in most games, as long as the catcher can throw out the faster runners, as long as the batter can hit .300 and drive in 100 runs per season, behavior does not matter. So it goes in baseball—and in much of the rest of life.

What becomes fearsome is when such childish attitudes are cherished in the church. Success at any price can never become an acceptable slogan—not for Christians. Our spiritual *success* is achieved by the *gifts* of the Spirit. They are the way God gets his work done through us. Our spiritual *attitude* is shaped by the *fruit* of the Spirit; it is the way God forms his character within us.

Fruit and gifts, gifts and fruit—this combination is difficult to come by. It puts us in direct conflict with the world's system of values which places a high price on success and a low one on character. Yet this combination of spiritual assets—gifts and fruit—is utterly essential for us to gain the holy balance that God intends for his church and its members. This worldly conflict and this holy balance are the two main points that need looking at if we are to understand how God uses the fruit of his Spirit alongside his gifts.

*The Worldly Conflict*

Achievement, attainment, acquisition, recognition— that quartet of ambitions sums up a lot of what we value in our world. *Success at any price* has become our silent slogan. Silent, I say, because we do not placard it on the bulletin boards of our offices or wear it **118** as a lapel pin on our jackets. Yet we live as though that were our motto. In fact, there is a whole genre of books that teach us how to be more aggressive, how to get our own way, how to climb to the top in our business or profession.

The sharp looking, nattily dressed young man sighed as he buckled himself into the airplane seat beside me. He should have been relieved because he was headed home after a week's absence. But he was not. He was loaded to the throat with anxiety. His home was filled with tension. He wanted to clamber to the presidency of his company; his wife could not care less whether he was number one or not. She was committed to her roomful of school kids whom she taught—and to her own family. Her husband's craving to climb to the top of the mountain was a foreign emotion to her. She was satisfied with a whole lot less.

He seemed a bit startled when I put the obvious question to him, "What is at the top?" "More challenge, I guess," was his rather lame reply. Here he was—and there are countless thousands like him—spending his health, jeopardizing his family, competing with his colleagues, outwitting his competitors with one aim in mind: to become president of the company. And he scarcely acknowledged the fact that, in his steely-eyed dedication to his work, history was repeating itself. His father was a distinguished surgeon and university professor. "Is your father proud of your success?" I asked him. "I'm not sure. My father and I are not close. He was always too busy pursuing his career." History was repeating itself in an assault on success whatever the cost.

The worldly ambition capsulated in that brief encounter on the airplane is an ever present danger to God's people. The negative characteristics of that way **119** of life we must shun as we would an epidemic of cholera. Success at any cost is a fatal formula, with its perverted priorities, its ruptured relations, its contorted characteristics. It can bring out the worst in us— selfishness, neglect of loved ones, impatience, dishonesty, even ruthlessness. Though these descriptions are never used at the promotion banquets of successful people, they are often more accurate than the terms that are used.

The worldly conflict is just this: the secular motto of success at any cost is at odds constantly with the biblical call to *character on God's terms.* God is not against success. He has done things well, ever since the first day of creation when he called his work good. But success that results in evil character traits, strained friendships, and broken marriage covenants is not true success.

Success on God's terms means one thing more than any other: becoming like him. God's aim for us often puts us in sharp conflict with the world. The world says, "Decide what you want in life and go after it with everything you've got." God says, "I want you to love me and live like me in righteousness and love."

We want to catch the connection between this worldly conflict and our use of the Spirit's gifts. The gifts of service, power, leadership, and stewardship are one key to spiritual success. But that one key cannot open the treasure chest by itself. God has designed his program like a safety-deposit box. Two keys are needed to open it. The depositor has her key and the banker has his key. Neither key alone can open the combination. It takes both keys together. In just the same way, spiritual success takes two keys: the Spirit's gifts and the Spirit's fruit. It is the combination of both these works of the Spirit that we call the holy **120** balance. It is God's solution to the worldly conflict.

*The Holy Balance*

The gifts of the Spirit have to do with *mission;* they are the God-given, God-empowered means of getting his work done through his church. The fruit of the Spirit have to do with *character;* they are the God-inspired, and God-implemented means of making God's people more like him.

Which of these is more important—gifts or fruit, mission or character? An impossible question to answer. God commands both; God enables us to participate in both. Above all he wants from his people the holy balance.

Gifts which push for spiritual success can be used harshly, proudly, and rashly, without the fruits of Christian personhood. Fruit, on the other hand, without the gifts can lead to isolationism, self-centeredness, and inactivity. Neither God nor we can settle for anything less than both.

*God wants to work through us.* To do so he has given each of his people at least one gift. These gifts, when used together in the Christian congregation, form a great dynamo of spiritual power for calling men and women to faith in Jesus and to growth in the new life that he alone can give. The multiplied and magnificent ways in which the gifts work have been the theme of most of the chapters in this book. We need not pause to review them here. It is enough to say that God is using our spiritual gifts to form a great people in every tongue and tribe and nation—to worship him, to serve each other, and to urge others to do the same.

*God wants to work in us,* as well as through us. This holy balance tells us that we are not just conduits through which spiritual power flows; we are not just channels bearing water to a thirsty land; we are not just tools building the house of God. Electric circuits, **121** irrigation canals, and skill saws all do their work effectively without being changed as they do it.

We are persons whom God designs to renew even while he is putting us to work. The Spirit works through us to change other lives while he works in us to make us better than we are.

This change of character the Bible describes as fruit. Paul gave us a list of nine characteristics which we Christians should demonstrate as the Spirit helps us do so: "But the fruit of the Spirit is love, joy, peace, patience, kindness, goodness, faithfulness, gentleness, self-control" (Galatians 5:22–23). No sensible person could vote against any of those—and happy is the soul whose neighbor possesses most of them!

The first three character traits—love, joy, peace— can be thought of as *responses to God's grace.* They capture the wonder of Christian freedom. The great truth that God has loved us through Jesus Christ and has called us to be part of his family has the power of a magnificent liberation. We have been thoroughly loved and from that love we can find strength to love. We have been mightily rescued and that rescue fills our spirits with joy. We have entered into full friendship with God, and that friendship conveys an imperturbable peace.

The next three traits—patience, kindness, goodness—can be viewed as *responses to the needs of others.* God's grace rebukes our selfishness and replaces it with love; it lifts our depression and infuses us with joy; it scatters our hostility and anxiety and sows in us the seed of peace. It also changes our behavior as it affects other people. Shortness of temper gives way to the kind of patience and longsuffering that God has shown us; harshness is sent scurrying by the type

122    of kindness and concern that God has lavished on us

through the compassionate Christ; selfishness is crowded out by the brand of goodness and generosity that God has demonstrated to his people through the ages.

The last three traits—faithfulness, gentleness, self-control—can be described as *attitudes of inner discipline.* They underscore the difference that the Holy Spirit can make in our character: instability and dishonesty are sent marching, and faithfulness and reliability take their place; ambition and aggressiveness are driven out, and gentleness and humility move in; temper and greed are shoved aside, and self-control and poise take over.

From all of this, we can see that the fruit of the Spirit are not mere decoration to make God's mission more pleasant. They are essential to that mission. God is not just gathering people to name his name; he is calling each of us to bear his character.

His aim is not success at any price, but mission on his terms. He is working toward community not competition. Teamwork among all of his people, not squabbling as to who is the most gifted superstar, is what he desires. Let the world do its quarreling, its boasting, its grasping for achievement. That worldly conflict the church does not need. God's holy balance is the more excellent way. We receive with gratitude his gifts and seek to use them daily. We cultivate with prayer and dedication his fruit and pray that God will make us more like him.

As gifts and fruit combine to accomplish his perfect work, the Creator-Redeemer Lord will again say, "Very good." That verdict is success in highest measure.

# Study Guide
# for
# Unwrapping Your
# Spiritual Gifts

**Chapter 1**
James 1:16–18

1. Is there a particular moment to which you can look back in your life when you remember unwrapping your gift(s) from the Giver? What were the reactions of you yourself, your family, and your friends?

2. What have been the significant steps you have taken in the unwrapping of your gifts? How is that unwrapping going on right now?

3. What doubts do you still have about whether you have discovered a spiritual gift? How can you deal with these uncertainties?

4. Jesus Christ is God's good and perfect gift to women and men. As "a kind of first fruits of his creatures,"

how are gifts a reflection of the Giver and his image? Compare James 1:18. Since their source is the "Father of Lights," what are some of the ways in which gifts illuminate our lives and our work?

## Chapter 2
1 Corinthians 12:4–7

1. How have you defined your spiritual gift or gifts? What difference has the discovery made in your life? Reflect upon your personal experience as it relates to this.

2. In what ways would the Church be the loser should your gift not be employed?

3. How does your gift cooperate with God's mission to serve "the common good" (1 Corinthians 12:7)?

4. To which category would you generally ascribe your gift—as generally a gift for service (Romans 12), leadership (Ephesians 4), power (1 Corinthians 12), or stewardship (1 Peter 4)? If you think you have a gift not on this list, do not be surprised. Chapters 9 and 10 may help explain why.

## Chapter 3
1 Corinthians 9:15–18

1. Looking back over your life, are there particular crises or events which helped shape your call? How can a call to be a steward of one's gift of grace be compared with a Damascus road-like call to conversion?

2. Are there particular needs you have witnessed which demand a sense of urgency, direction, and **125**

obligation? Consider 1 Corinthians 9:16–18, where Paul's sense of call—"Woe to me . . ."—is keenly felt.

3. What do you like to do? Where do you have particular abilities? Which needs are you best suited to help meet?

4. Can we always assume a close relationship between one's talent and one's call? See also Chapter 10.

**Chapter 4**
Romans 12:3–8

1. How did your commitment to Christ change your perspective on your abilities and gifts?

2. Can any of the gifts listed in Romans 12:3–8 of prophecy, service, teaching, exhortation, contributing, giving aid, and acts of mercy be applied to describe your own abilities? Who are some members of your church who exercise these gifts?

3. What do spiritual gifts tell us about God's character? What do they tell you about yourself?

4. I suggest that teaching is one gift which virtually every believer should give a test. Are there gifts which you have tested during the course of your pilgrimage, and which you subsequently no longer pursue? If so, why?

5. In Romans 12:3–5, Paul exhorts each reader of his letter "not to think of himself more highly than he ought to think, but to think with sober judgment, each according to the measure of faith which God

has assigned him." He goes on, in verses 4 and 5, to state that "as in one body we have many members, and all the members do not have the same function, so we, though many, are one body in Christ, and individually members one of another." What is the relationship between these two sets of statements in verse 3 and in verses 4 and 5?

**Chapter 5**
1 Corinthians 12:4–11

1. Of what assistance is the rest of the body of Christ in discerning your spiritual gifts? Is their process of discernment a formal or informal one? What do your pastor and other leaders do to encourage the discovery of gifts?

2. What people in your church fellowship are able sensitively to evaluate, critique, and hold you accountable for your gift and its employment? How do they do this?

3. Imagine yourself in a court of law. You are asked by the prosecuting attorney to produce evidence supporting your claim that you have a particular spiritual gift. What evidence can you cite? What scripture can you quote which supports the exercise of your gift? Who is able to testify as a witness on your behalf?

4. Gifts of service, which we looked at in Chapter 4, are perhaps more familiar to you than are such gifts of power as speaking in tongues, working miracles, and healing the sick listed in 1 Corinthians 12:4–11. What has been your personal experience with **127**

such "power-oriented" gifts of the Spirit? What about close friends or family members?

5. What may be the particular roles that such gifts of power may play in the work of God's kingdom?

**Chapter 6**
Ephesians 4:11–16

1. How has the leadership of your church shepherded and instructed its members, and particularly you, in the gifts of the Spirit?

2. In your church or denomination, how are leaders such as pastor-teachers and evangelists chosen?

3. Why, according to James, are teachers judged more severely in the exercise of their gifts? How can the same admonition be applied to leaders in general?

4. If your gifts call you to some form of leadership, which people have served as models for you within the church?

5. Have you ever had to wrestle with other people's perceptions of what your gifts are, and your own personal conviction that your gifts are quite different from their opinion? How should we reconcile this kind of conflict?

6. In Ephesians 4:15b–16, Paul admonishes his hearers to "grow up in every way into him who is the head, into Christ, from whom the whole body, joined and knit together by every joint with which it is supplied, when each part is working properly, makes

bodily growth and upbuilds itself in love." Is there a part of your physical body which can be compared to your spiritual gift?

## Chapter 7
1 Peter 4:7–11

1. Many of us, realizing all that life requires, know we cannot do everything we are asked or called upon to do. As exciting and as challenging as the employment of your gift may be, using it may sometimes come at the expense of other abilities and talents. What have you had to sacrifice for the sake of your gift? What personal conflicts within you has your gift provoked?

2. Upon recognition of your gifts, were you encouraged to seek any sort of special training to help develop and empower them? If you only recently discovered your gifts, how are you planning to develop them?

3. In what way is the exercise of your gift an act of service? Of sacrifice? A manifestation of God's glory through Jesus Christ?

4. Cultivating your spiritual gifts takes more than the training and practice at *doing;* it takes training and practice at *being.* What is the relation between your *being* as a spiritual person, and the *doing* of your spiritual gifts? See also Chapter 11.

5. Define the meaning and importance of hospitality as a means of extending God's grace today. Compare 1 Peter 4:9.

## Chapter 8
Matthew 25:14–30

1. Imagine your spiritual gift as one of Jesus' own precious properties, given to you. In what way does he hold us accountable for the given talent? How does the Church hold us accountable?

2. In the parable of the talents, the man who had been given the one talent and who had not multiplied what he had been given had it forfeited by God, to the accompaniment of some very harsh words. Why is such a drastic response on God's part necessary? Compare Matthew 25:26–30.

3. Have you ever been tempted to hide your "one talent," and if so, why?

4. What evidence is there that God's precious investment in us has paid interest? How have you multiplied the talents you have been given? Describe what you think an unmultiplied talent might look like.

5. Have you been faithful over the little God has given? Jesus suggests that if a servant has been faithful over a little he will then be set over much. What does he mean by this? What are the marks of a faithful and diligent employment of one's gift?

## Chapter 9
Acts 1:6–11

1. During the course of this book and study, we have
had the opportunity to look at the four great New

Testament lists of gifts—gifts of service (Romans 12), gifts of power (1 Corinthians 12), gifts of leadership (Ephesians 4), and gifts of stewardship (1 Peter 4). What might be an example of a spiritual gift which the Bible does not specifically mention, but which you have witnessed in the life of the Church? How does this relate to the Holy Spirit's work?

2. Are there other members of the church with gifts similar to yours who serve as an inspiration or model for you?

3. In what ways do you enjoy the gift God has given to you?

**Chapter 10**
Psalm 139:13–18

1. Is there a mysterious element to the link between you and your gift? What is it?

2. How have your heredity, environment, and other factors prepared you for your gifts? How have these contributed to the building of a foundation upon which your life and gifts are exercised?

3. Think for a moment about the history of your own life and how the details have dovetailed to create the whole. How does the scope of your life history contribute to your present sense of confidence and commitment?

**Chapter 11**
Galatians 5:22–24

1. The gifts God has given his people are exciting, and for many, the employment of them is consum-    **131**

ing. How does worldly ambition differ from our ambition to serve God with our gifts?

2. How do we keep the zealous employment of one's gift in check with other responsibilities, such as health and family? If there needs to be a line drawn as to limits, where are the lines drawn, and how are these decisions made?

3. The gifts of the Spirit have to do with mission and the fruits of the Spirit have to do with character. How does the fruit of the Spirit inform and balance the exercise of your spiritual gifts?

4. Do your family and Christian community encourage you in the exercise of your gifts? How do they help you draw, or undraw, the lines?

5. How confident are you that God wants to work through you?

6. What more are you asking God's Spirit to do in your life?